Evangelista's

NEW MEXICAN

COOKBOOK

Spice up your life

Evangelista's
NEW MEXICAN
COOKBOOK

Ruben Evangelista

J & B Editions, Publishers

Distributed by:

Hampton Roads Publishing Company, Inc.
891 Norfolk Square
Norfolk, VA 23502

If this book isn't available from your bookseller, it may be obtained directly from the publisher or distributor. Call toll-free 1-800-766-8009 (orders only).

ISBN 1-878901-16-8

10 9 8 7 6 5 4 3 2 1

Credit References:

Betty Crocker's Southwest Cookery. New York: Prentice Hall, 1989.
Butel, Jane. *Chili Madness*. New York: Workman Publishing, 1981.
Murphy, Rosalea. *The Pink Adobe Cookbook*. New York: Dell Publishing, 1988.
Quintana, Patricia. *The Taste of Mexico*. New York: Stewart, Tabori, & Chang, 1986.
Stern, Jane and Michael. "Annals of Gastronomy, Chilies," *The New Yorker*, May 25, 1992.

Printed in the United States of America

For my Dad

Death Ends A Life But Not A Relationship

I dedicate this labor of love to my father who taught me to be creative and experiment with all foods.

Sometimes I feel as if I'm an artist and my canvas is a plain white plate; there are no new colors or foods, just new ways of mixing and arranging them. Dad, I hope you are pleased. You've taught me everything I now know; however, I must still learn everything you knew.

Also to Kathy, my loving wife and my inspiration, the true driving force behind our successful restaurant, and especially this book: you bring out the best in me.

And to my son Antonio, who works at my side and shows the same passion and imagination for food I remember most about my Dad.

And to my daughter Shelly, whose smile would brighten anyone and everyone's day. Shelly always says everything is great and makes one feel that it's true.

To all of our many, many guests who believed in us and frequented Lista's many times a week, we know that you would say, "We must go in there or they're not going to make it." Often, you were the only people to cross our threshold on cold wintry evenings, just to keep Kathy and me company. We remember those times well. Thank you for being there.

INTRODUCCIÓN

Dear Readers,

My wife, Kathy, and I invite you to read and use *EvangeLista's New Mexican Cookbook*. We want to share a little secret with you. You aren't sampling Mexican food, you're feasting on *New Mexican* cuisine. The distinction may be minor, but to us it's important. Not many people realize that Southwestern food is an indigenous part of American cuisine. The New Mexico region has been influenced by many different cultures — Spanish, Native American, Mexican, Texan, even Cajun and Creole — variations of all of them are present in the traditional foods of the state of New Mexico.

Mexican-style cooking has long been a favorite cuisine of Americans for many years. Lista's has concentrated on the upscale Mexican-style with inclusion of a vast variety of fresh ingredients — everything from apples to zucchini and every type of shellfish, poultry, and red meat available. While we have given canned and frozen alternatives for fresh ingredients in many of the recipes, please remember that much of the freshness, color, and crispness in texture will suffer.

The same rule applies when a salsa or sauce is called for from another recipe. Many supermarkets and specialty food stores have a variety of good ingredients — prepared sauces, flour or corn tortillas, chorizo sausage, fresh and dried spices.

Most early New Mexican recipes were built around tortillas, chiles, beans, and meat — about the only ingredients available to cooks in the early days of the Santa Fe trail; however, this dearth of ingredients was actually a blessing. It inspired endless creativity to invent variations of the same foods. Today this creative spirit is still alive — and we have varied ingredients to make the food taste even better. Southwestern cuisine is bold, flavorful, remarkably healthy, full of fresh vegetables, grains, and legumes, and prepared with very little fat or salt.

I learned to love this food as a child, growing up in the northern New Mexico-southern Colorado area. My father was a professional chef and many of my favorite recipes were learned at his side.

When using this book, please do not hesitate to be creative. Creativity in the kitchen is a true art; after practicing basic techniques, be adventurous and experiment. Let your own style surface and then each delicious creation will be your own.

The first thing my father, Florencio Perez Evangelista (how's that for a name with some personality?), taught me is that you cannot make bad food taste good. Start with quality ingredients. At the restaurant, we use only fresh vegetables and fruit, certified Angus beef, milk-fed veal, and the finest poultry available. Since we are located on the East Coast, we take advantage of the availability of local seafood.

Use fresh seafood if it is available. Whether fresh or frozen, use the best quality. With the ability to cut clean and pack under government supervision, even quick-freeze on board ship is better than holding seafood in water or ice. Remember, many fishing boats are out for days at a time, and product labeled "fresh" is not always fresh.

All good chefs and cooks insist on high quality in all aspects of cooking. Again, try to use fresh foods and, when in doubt, use the best. Ask for help in any particular section of your supermarket or specialty food store. At Lista's, we have never chosen lower price before quality. However, many recipes in this book will prove to be inexpensive.

Kathy and I hope that you'll enjoy preparing the recipes from *EvangeLista's New Mexican Cookbook* as much as we enjoy serving them to our patrons.

Bon appetito!

TABLE OF CONTENTS

There is an old saying about peppers or chiles: "If you see the angels after tasting the tip of them — proceed and eat or use them in cooking; however, if you see god — eat or use only half the amount!"

Identification of Chile Peppers and their Degree of Hotness
(Scale of 1 to 10: mild to hot)

AJÍ MIRASOL. (Also: Kellu-Uchu, Ají Amarillo). Source: South America. Ingredient in yellow moles and ceviches and salsas. Berry Flavor. (2.5)

AJIPANCA. Source: Peru. Makes a good addition to chile sauces and fish dishes. (1.5)

ANCHO. Dried Poblano. Source: Puebla region. Sweetest of the chiles. Ideal for sauces and moles. (4.5)

CASACABEL: Source: Central Mexico. Name means "little rattle." Seeds rattle when shaken. Used in salsas, sauces and soups. (4)

CATARINA. Source: Central and Northern Mexico, Southern Texas. Seeds rattle when shaken. Ideal for spicy salsas and soups. (4)

CAYENNE. Source: Louisiana, Mexico, Asia, Africa, Japan. Mainly a powder for seasoning. (9-10)

CHILHUACLE AMARILLO. Source: Oaxaca only. Most commonly used in yellow moles and other sauces. (4)

CHIHUACLE NEGRO. Source: Only in Oaxaca. Rare and unique flavor. Ideal for black moles. (5)

CHIHUACLE ROJO: (Also: de Colorado). Source: Oaxaca only. Used in special moles. (4)

CHILCOSLE. (Also: Amarillo). Source: Oaxaca. Primarily used in salsas, tamales, and soups. (5.5)

CHILE SECO. (Dried Serrano). Source: Veracruz and Central Mexican Valley. Used mainly as powder, in salsas. (7.5)

CHILE SECO DE YUCATAN. Dried Serrano. Source: Yucatán and Veracruz. Used as powdered seasoning or mixed with other spices. (5)

CHILTEPE. Source: Oaxaca. Excellent seasoning for sauces. (6)

CHIPOTLE: (Also: Abumado). Dried smoked Jalapeño. Source: Mexico, Rio Grande Valley, Best in seasonings and soups. (6)

CHIPOTLE GRANDE. (Also: Oaxaca Navideño). Smoked. Rare and expensive. Source: Puebla and Oaxaca regions. Excellent seasoning for meats and sauces. (5)

COSTEÑO. (Also: Bandeño). A type of Guajillo. Source: Guerrero and Oaxaca. Commonly used in salsas and sauces. (5.5)

Continued on Page 12

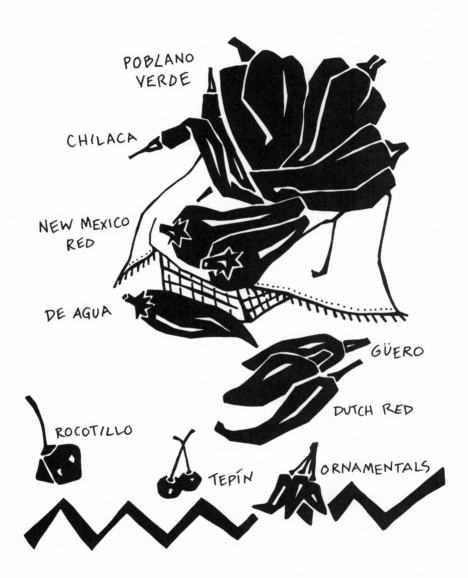

POBLANO VERDE

CHILACA

NEW MEXICO RED

DE AGUA

GÜERO

DUTCH RED

ROCOTILLO

TEPÍN

ORNAMENTALS

Continuation of Chile Pepper Identification

COSTEÑO DE AMARILLO. Source: Oaxaca. Mainly used in yellow moles. (4)

DE AROBL. Related to Cayenne and Guajillo. Source: Northern and Central Mexico. Soaked and used in sauces. (8)

GUAJILLO. (Also: Mirasol). Source: Northern and Central Mexico. Mainly for enchiladas, salsas, and dried chile sauces. (4-5)

MORA. (Also: Mora Rojo). Type of Jalapeño. Smoked. Source: Northern and Central Mexico. Used in salsas and sauces. (5.5)

MORITA. A small Mora, type, of Jalapeño. Smoked. Source: Central Mexican Valley. Used in Salsas and sauces. (6.5)

MULATO. Dried ripe Poblano. Source: Central Mexico. Best in moles and either dried chile sauce (1)

NEW MEXICO BROWN. (Eclipse) Source and uses same as New Mexico Yellow. (2-3)

NEW MEXICO GREEN. (Also: California). Source: Rio Grande Valley. Roasted, peeled, and mainly used in stews, sometimes powdered, used for making beef jerky. (5)

NEW MEXICO ORANGE. (Sunset). Source and uses same as New Mexico Yellow. (2-3)

NEW MEXICO RED. (Also: Colorado, California). Source: Rio Grande Valley. Whole and powdered. Excellent for traditional sauces and salsas. (3-4)

NEW MEXICO YELLOW. (Sunrise). Source: Rio Grande Valley. Ornamental. Used mainly as decoration in ristras. (2-3)

ONZA. Source: Oaxaca only Very rare. Makes a good addition to sauces and soups. (4)

PASILLA. (Also: Chile Negro). Dried Chilaca. Source: Central Mexican Valley. Used in sauces and moles. (3-4)

PASILLA DE OAXACA. Smoked. Source: Oaxaca. Used mainly for rellenos (regional specialty). (6)

PEPPERONCINI. Source: Sardinia and Southern Italy. used in flavoring tomato sauces and seafood dishes. (5)

PEQUÍN. Source: Northern Mexico, the Southwest. Ideal in salsas and vinegars. (8.5)

PICO DE PAJARO. Name means "bird's beak." Source: Northern and Central Mexico. Used in pickling and marinades. (6-7)

PUYA (or PUILLIA). A type of Guajillo. Source: Central Mexican Valley. Excellent seasoning for salsas and stews. (6)

TEPIN. (Also: Chiltepín). Source: N. Mexico, the Southwest. Wild chile, used mainly in flavored vinegars and prized for its flavor in salsas. (8)

ANTOJITOS
y
BOTANAS

Antojitos
(Little Whims)
16 Antojitos, 4 to 5 appetizer servings

Antojitos have been a favorite starter at Lista's. These little chimis can be filled with just about anything, from refried beans and cheese to shredded beef with red chile. Try fruit or pie fillings for an after-dinner treat.

2 tablespoons butter or margarine
4 large thin flour tortillas, (*each* at least 12 inches in diameter)
1 stalk broccoli, chopped into *very* small pieces, including
  florets and stems
1/4 cup minced peeled onion
1/4 cup shredded Monterey Jack cheese
16 small wooden picks
Approximately 2 cups cooking oil for frying
Salsa of choice or Lista's Guacamole (see index)

Melt butter or margarine in a non-stick medium heavy skillet over moderate heat. Add broccoli and onion; sauté quickly until tender but not soft or mushy. Add cheese, stirring constantly. Remove from heat and allow to cool. Cut flour tortillas into fourths; place about 1 tablespoon broccoli-onion-cheese mixture in the center of *each* tortilla (with the rounded side of *each* placed toward you). Fold *each* side inward; then roll the last corner up tightly and secure with a wooden pick. In a deep fryer, heat oil to about medium (325°F.). Using tongs, deep-fry 4 to 6 chimis at a time, turning occasionally. Deep-fry to a golden brown color, about 2 minutes. Serve with a mild salsa or Lista's Guacamole.

Camarónes Ajillo
(Garlic Shrimp)
2 appetizer servings

For best results use a cast-iron skillet — just warmed, not hot.

8 ounces large (*36 to 40-count*) shrimp, peeled and deveined (see note)
1/4 cup *extra virgin* olive oil
1/4 cup butter or margarine
2 tablespoons minced peeled garlic
1/2 teaspoon crushed dried chile pequin or crushed dried
  hot red pepper
1 tablespoon minced *fresh* cilantro or parsley
1 1/2 to 2 tablespoons *fresh* lemon juice
Sprigs of *fresh* cilantro or parsley and thin lemon wedges for garnish.

Add olive oil, butter, garlic, and chile pequin to a warm medium heavy skillet, stirring constantly until butter is melted. Increase heat and quickly stir-fry shrimp about 5 minutes, or until shrimp are opaque and coral pink in color. Sprinkle cilantro or parsley over shrimp; add lemon juice, mixing gently. Drain, reserving sauce for dipping. Serve immediately. Garnish with sprigs of cilantro or parsley and lemon wedges, if desired. Pass the sauce for dipping shrimp.

Note: Shrimp may be butterflied, if desired. To butterfly, slit each shrimp lengthwise down the inside center of the shrimp with a sharp knife, cutting each almost through. Shrimp will open out flat but remain joined at the center.

Cantina Nuts
2 cups

These nuts started as a snack for a few regular patrons of our cantina. My imagination has led me to use the tasty peanuts in many recipes. Try fresh spinach and onion sautéed in our house dressing with the addition of nuts — or Molé Poblana. Hmmm — good! They also are perfect with beer.

1 tablespoon peanut oil
2 cups lightly salted peanuts
1 teaspoon New Mexican-style (bright red) chili powder

In a teflon-coated medium heavy skillet, heat oil. Add peanuts; sauté, stirring constantly, over moderate heat for 3 to 5 minutes, *being careful not to burn nuts*. When peanuts are hot, add chili powder; continue to sauté, stirring and shaking pan constantly for 2 minutes. Remove from heat; drain well. Serve hot or at room temperature.

Macho Nachos
(Rugged Snacks)
3 to 4 appetizer servings

Crisp corn chips, approximately 30 pieces
1 cup Frijóles Refritos (refried beans) (see index)
5 1/2 ounces (about 1 1/3 cups) shredded sharp Cheddar or
  Monterey Jack cheese
1/4 cup Lista's Guacamole (see index)
1/4 cup sour cream
1/4 cup chopped firm *ripe* tomato
2 tablespoons thinly sliced jalapeño chile peppers
2 tablespoons thinly sliced green onions (scallions) (include some
  green tops)

Arrange corn chips on a large oven-proof plate or medium oven-proof platter. Evenly sprinkle or spread refried beans over chips. Top with cheese, dividing evenly. Bake in a preheated slow oven (325°F.) for about 5 minutes, or until cheese is melted. In order, top hot nachos with Lista's Guacamole, sour cream, tomatoes, jalapeño peppers, and green onions. Serve immediately.

Ceviche de Mariscos
(Marinated Seafood)
4 appetizer servings

Most ceviche recipes use seafood, whatever variety available; however, at Lista's, we use gently cooked fish and shellfish.

4 cups water
4 ounces bay scallops (see note)
4 ounces whitefish fillets, cut into small pieces
1 *fresh* jalapeño chile pepper, minced, seeds discarded
1/4 cup *fresh* lime juice
1/4 cup minced peeled onion
1 teaspoon minced *fresh* cilantro or parsley
1/2 teaspoon salt or to taste
1/4 teaspoon minced peeled garlic
1/4 teaspoon white pepper or to taste
1/4 teaspoon seafood seasoning (see note)
4 ounces crabmeat (see note)
2 *ripe* medium avocados, peeled, pitted, halved,
and immediately sprinkled with lemon or lime juice *fresh* lime wedges
and sprigs of cilantro or parsley for garnish

In a 3-quart heavy saucepan, bring water to a boil over high heat. Combine scallops, whitefish, jalapeño pepper, lime juice, onion, minced cilantro, salt, garlic, pepper, and seafood seasoning, mixing lightly. Add mixture to boiling water, stirring constantly; reduce heat and simmer for 3 to 5 minutes. Drain well, transfer to a bowl, and add crabmeat; cover and allow to chill in the refrigerator for 12 hours. Prepare avocados. Fill *each* half with seafood mixture, dividing evenly. Serve with *fresh* lime.

Note: Bay scallops are the very tender small scallops from the Chesapeake or Cape Cod bays. May substitute small sea scallops, if desired.

Note: Preferably use Old Bay brand seafood seasoning.

Note: Pick over crabmeat, removing any shell or cartilage.

Chile con Queso
(Melted Cheese with Chile Peppers)
6 to 8 appetizer servings

There are many prepared cheese sauces; some have jalapeños in them. If you spice them up just a bit more using your own creative cooking skills, you can call them your own. Here is one of mine, which I serve with crisp flour tortillas chips. It also makes an excellent fondue in which to dip fresh pear and apple wedges.

2 hot-spiced green chile peppers or jalapeño chile peppers, minced
1 cup shredded mild Cheddar cheese
1 cup shredded Monterey Jack cheese

1/2 cup minced peeled onion
1/2 cup chopped firm *ripe* tomato
1/4 cup pitted black olives, drained and minced
1/4 cup milk or heavy cream
1/2 teaspoon minced peeled garlic
1/2 teaspoon white pepper or to taste
Pinch of minced *fresh* cilantro or parsley
Pinch of minced *fresh* oregano
Crisp flour or corn tortilla chips as dippers

Combine all ingredients in a non-stick large heavy skillet over low to moderate heat, stirring constantly, until mixture is smooth and no longer stringy. Transfer to a serving dish and serve with crisp flour or corn tortilla chips.

Chili con Queso Another Way
(Melted Cheese with Chile Peppers Another Way)
6 appetizer servings

1 cup (4 ounces) shredded Monterey Jack cheese
1/3 cup Lista's Enchilada Sauce (see index)
2 tablespoons Pico de Gallo (see index)
Crisp flour tortilla triangles as desired

In a medium heavy saucepan, combine the first 3 ingredients. Cook over low heat, stirring frequently, until cheese is melted and mixture is smooth, about 5 minutes. Serve hot accompanied with flour tortilla triangles as dippers.

Southwestern Bean Dip
10 to 12 appetizer servings

This recipe is easy to prepare — a quick idea to entertain guests during a football game or as an afternoon snack by the pool.

3 cups prepared Frijóles Refritos (refried beans) (see index) or
    1 (16-ounce) can
Water as needed
1 cup Picante Sauce or Salsa Verde (see index)
1 cup shredded sharp Cheddar or Monterey Jack cheese
1/4 cup thinly sliced green onions (scallions) (include some green tops)
Crisp corn or flour tortilla chips as desired

Warm refried beans in a non-stick medium heavy skillet over low to moderate heat; add enough water to make mixture almost runny. Add Picante Sauce and cheese, mixing constantly, until smooth. Transfer to a serving bowl, garnish with onions, and accompany with crisp corn or flour tortilla chips as dippers.

Crabmeat and Broccoli Nachos
(Crabmeat and Broccoli Snacks)
4 to 6 appetizer servings

4 ounces backfin crabmeat
4 ounces crisp corn chips
2 tablespoons butter or margarine
4 ounces chopped broccoli (including florets and tender stems)
2 tablespoons water
2 tablespoons chopped peeled onion
5 1/2 ounces (about 1 1/3 cups) shredded Monterey Jack cheese
2 tablespoons minced peeled mild green chile peppers or jalapeño
    chile peppers
2 tablespoons heavy cream (optional)
Freshly ground black pepper to taste
Thinly sliced pitted black olives and green onions (scallions)
    for garnish (include some green tops)

Pick over crabmeat, removing any shell or cartilage; set aside. Pile corn chips on a large oven-proof plate; set aside. In a non-stick large heavy skillet, melt butter over moderate heat; add broccoli and water. Sauté for 2 minutes. Add onion and sauté again until vegetables are tender, about 2 minutes. Add remaining ingredients, stirring constantly, until cheese is melted and smooth in consistency. Pour mixture over chips. Garnish with sliced olives and/or green onions, if desired. Serve immediately.

Lista's Guacamole
(Avocado Appetizer)
6 to 10 appetizer servings

3 *ripe* large avocados (see note)
Lime juice as desired
1/2 cup chopped peeled onion
2 tablespoons minced jalapeño chile pepper (see note)
1/2 teaspoon chopped peeled garlic
1/2 teaspoon salt or to taste
1/4 teaspoon freshly ground black pepper
1/2 cup chopped firm *ripe* tomato
Crisp corn chips as dippers

With a sharp knife, cut avocados in half lengthwise; remove peel and seeds. Immediately sprinkle with lime juice to prevent discoloration of avocados. In a medium bowl, thoroughly mash avocados with a potato masher or a fork. Add jalapeño peppers, garlic, salt, and pepper, mixing well. Add tomatoes, if desired, mixing gently. Or, sprinkle over the surface of the spread as a garnish. Spoon guacamole into the center of a large serving platter and surround with crisp corn chips as dippers.

Note: The avocado seed may be immersed in the guacamole spread to prevent discoloration from occurring.

Note: Fresh or canned jalapeño chile peppers, but not pickled peppers, may be used.

Lobster Flan
(Lobster Custard)
6 appetizer servings

Flan is usually a dessert; however, leaving out the sweetness and adding a little imagination, it becomes an appetizer.

6 eggs, at room temperature
2 cups milk
1/2 teaspoon vanilla extract
1 cup cut-up cooked lobster, cut into bite-size pieces (see note)
1/3 cup sugar

In a 3-quart heavy saucepan, beat eggs lightly with a wire whisk; add milk. Cook, stirring constantly, over low to moderate heat until mixture coats a spoon and thickens slightly. Remove from heat. Add lobster and vanilla, mixing lightly; set aside. In a small heavy skillet, melt sugar, stirring constantly, over moderate heat; continue to stir over heat until sugar turns a light caramel color. Spoon hot caramelized syrup into 6 individual heatproof, 1-cup, 4 1/2-inch diameter, glass baking cups, dividing evenly. Spoon lobster-custard mixture into *each*, dividing evenly. Chill custards in the refrigerator until firm. To serve, run a rubber spatula around the rim of *each* flan (custard) to loosen; invert *each* onto an appetizer plate and tap the baking cup gently, allowing the flan to slide onto the plate, caramel syrup-side up. Garnish as desired.

Note: A 2 to 2 1/2-pound lobster will provide about 1 pound cooked meat or 1 cup cut-up cooked meat.

Mussels Verde
(Mussels with Green Chili Sauce)
6 appetizer servings

East meets Southwest in this recipe. Being from Colorado, I was totally unfamiliar with most seafood, especially mussels. Who was to know that these charcoal-colored shells with seaweed hanging from them held one of the tastiest bite-size morsels the seas have to offer. Top them off with Denver-style green chili. Aye, Aye, Aye!!!

1 cup water
24 to 40 mussels
1/4 cup minced *fresh* cilantro
1/4 cup lemon juice
3 cups Chili Verde (see index) or other prepared chili, heated through
Thin lemon wedges for garnish

In a large heavy saucepan, bring water to boiling over moderate heat. Arrange mussels on a rack that will fit into the saucepan *just* above the water level. Place mussels on rack in the saucepan. Sprinkle with cilantro and lemon juice; cover and steam over moderate heat for 6 to 8 minutes or until mussel shells open. Place mussels, including any liquid, in a large serving bowl. Ladle Chili Verde evenly over mussels and garnish with lemon wedges.

Basic Nachos
(Basic Crisp Tortilla Snacks)
2 appetizer servings

This favorite Mexican finger food can now be found on a variety of menus across the USA. There are many versions. Legend suggests that nachos were invented during World War II in south Texas by Egnacio, a harried restaurant proprietor, trying to feed a bunch of hungry boisterous Army Air Force pilots. To keep them happy while he prepared their dinners, Egnacio satisfied them with crisp fixed tortilla triangles topped with melted cheese and jalapeños. Of course, they were dubbed Nachos, the nickname of the owner.

8 to 10 round corn chips
4 ounces (1 cup) shredded Monterey Jack cheese
8 to 10 jalapeño chile pepper "wheel" slices
Lista's Guacamole (see index)

Arrange corn chips on an oven-proof plate or small platter. Evenly sprinkle cheese over chips, dividing evenly. Bake in a preheated moderate oven (350°F.) for about 8 to 10 minutes or until cheese is melted. Garnish with jalapeño pepper "wheel" slices and Lista's Guacamole, if desired. Serve immediately.

Nachos al Carbon
(Steak Snacks)
2 to 3 appetizer servings

4 ounces beef steak (flank, London Broil, or sirloin tip)
Garlic powder or juice to taste
Salt and freshly ground black pepper to taste
Basic Nachos (see page 20)

Sprinkle steak lightly with garlic powder or juice, salt, and pepper. Grill or broil, 6 to 8 inches from heat source, until beef is desired degree of doneness, about 2 to 3 minutes per side for medium rare. Or, charcoal grill, 8 to 10 inches above medium coals, (ash gray and glowing) until beef is done, abut 3 minutes per side. Or, sauté beef in a medium heavy skillet sprayed with non-stick vegetable cooking spray until beef is done. With a sharp knife, cut beef into 8 bite-size pieces. Place atop hot prepared Basic Nachos, dividing evenly. Serve immediately.

Note: See touch test for doneness of steak (page 39).

Botana is Spanish for starter or appetizer or hors d'oeuvre.

PB & J's
4 to 6 appetizer servings

Not peanut butter and jelly, but peanut butter and jalapeños! This is one of many dishes inspired by my wife, Kathy. It is zesty and flavorful, but not overpowering. These botanas really get your taste buds ready for a true southwestern feast.

6 firm large jalapeño chile peppers
Crisp red-tipped leaf lettuce as desired
6 tablespoons creamy or chunky-style peanut butter
1 large apple, cored, seeded, and cut into wedges

With a sharp knife, cut *each* jalapeño lengthwise in half. With a potato peeler or the small end of a teaspoon, remove the seeds and the membrane of *each* half. Arrange lettuce leaves on a large serving plate. Fill *each* jalapeño pepper half with peanut butter, dividing evenly; arrange filled jalapeño peppers over lettuce, stems pointing out. Arrange apple wedges between the stuffed jalapeños.

Quesadilla
(Cheese Crisp)
4 appetizer servings

The hardest part of the preparation of this recipe is heating the skillet to the correct temperature.

1 serrano chile pepper, thinly sliced
1/4 cup chopped firm *ripe* tomatoes
1/4 cup chopped peeled onions
1 teaspoon minced fresh cilantro
2 thin large flour tortillas, divided
1 1/2 cups shredded sharp Cheddar or Monterey Jack cheese
1 cup shredded iceberg lettuce
1/2 cup Lista's Guacamole (see index)
1/2 cup sour cream
Sliced pitted black olives as desired for garnish (optional)
Chopped green onions (scallions) as desired for garnish (optional)

In a small bowl, combine the first 4 ingredients. Preheat a large cast-iron skillet to hot; add one tortila and heat sligtly over moderate heat. Sprinkle cheese over tortilla in skillet; spread tomato mixture over cheese. Top with second tortilla and press down gently. Continue to heat until bottom tortilla becomes crisp and cheese melts; turn (over) Quesadilla to crisp second tortilla. Spread lettuce on a serving plate. Spoon guacamole and sour cream at one side of the plate. Cut hot Quesadilla into several equal-size pie-shaped pieces and arrange over the shredded lettuce. Garnish Quesadilla with sliced black olives and chopped green onions.

Scallops Aduvada
4 to 6 appetizer servings

Aduvada Sauce is one of Lista's favorite sauces, but remember it is very hot and will take some time and experimenting to learn how to use it comfortably. Don't let the word "hot" scare you away. The flavor it gives to scallops or shrimp wrapped in bacon is truly unbelievable and desirable.

12 large sea scallops
6 slices bacon, *each* cut in half
12 small wooden picks
1/4 cup prepared Salsa Aduvada (see index)
4 to 6 scallop shells or individual seafood baking dishes

Wrap a bacon half-slice around *each* scallop, securing *each* with a wooden pick. Arrange bacon wrapped scallops on a lightly greased 12 x 9-inch baking sheet; baste *each* liberally with Aduvada Sauce. Bake in a preheated moderate oven (350°F.) for 8 to 10 minutes or until scallops are opaque in color and can be cut easily with a fork. *Do not overbake as scallops will become tough.* Arrange in scallop shells or individual seafood baking dishes, garnish as desired, and serve immediately.

Taquitos
(Deep-Fried Rolled Small Tacos)
4 appetizer servings

In order to prepare these tasty tidbits, you will have to prepare shredded cooked beef or chicken. You may use leftovers such as pot roast or roast chicken. Preparing Taquitos could be a great way to get the "gang" to eat leftovers.

2 cups cooking oil for frying
8 ounces shredded cooked beef or chicken or Pulled or Shredded Beef or
   Pollo (Chicken) (see index)
8 corn tortillas
8 small wooden picks
Lista's Guacamole for garnish (see index)
Sour cream for garnish
Lista's Hot Sauce or Salsa Fresca for garnish (see index)

In a deep medium skillet, heat oil to medium (about 350°F.). (Oil will sputter when a few drops of water are sprinkled over hot oil.) Pan-fry *each* tortilla, one at a time, *just* until *each* tortilla is soft and pliable; transfer tortillas to absorbent paper to drain well and cool, but not harden. Divide shredded beef or chicken into *each* tortilla. Roll *each* tightly and secure with a wooden pick. Return rolled tortillas to hot oil in skillet and pan-fry until tortillas are crisp, turning frequently. Drain well on absorbent paper. Allow two taquitos per appetizer serving. Garnish *each* with Lista's Guacamole, sour cream, and Picante Sauce as desired.

Tostadas
(Layered Crispy Tortillas)
4 appetizer servings

Some of you may know these as chalupas. These tasty morsels may be topped with just about anything — refried beans, ground beef, chicken, guacamole, or black beans. It is your choice. As a child, my family would make these for lunch or dinner. Sometimes they would serve them as a snack. Your appetite will dictate the amount.

8 crisp-fried small flat corn tortillas, divided
4 cups Frijóles Refritos (refried beans) (see index) or cooked
**   black beans, divided**
1 head iceberg lettuce, shredded or torn into bite-size pieces, divided
6 ounces (1 1/2 cups) shredded sharp Cheddar or Monterey Jack
**   cheese, divided**
1 cup Lista's Hot Sauce or Salsa Fresca (see index), divided

Arrange two tortillas on *each* of four individual plates. Spread *each* tortilla with beans and then add lettuce, dividing evenly. Sprinkle *each* with grated cheese. Garnish with hot sauce as desired.

Kathy's Spinach and
Cream Cheese Quesadilla
4 servings

One of Lista's favorite appetizers has been Kathy's Spinach and Cream Cheese Quesadilla. It's light, yet so flavorful. You won't believe that it's very low in calories. Just like any thing else, you must practice to get the tortillas to crisp just a bit without the cream cheese oozing out the sides. Adjust the temperature. One trick is to start the tortilla on the grill or skillet first.

8 ounces *fresh* spinach
1 tablespoon *extra virgin* olive oil
4 (8 to 9-inch) flour tortillas
1 (8-ounce) package cream cheese, *just* at room temperature
1/2 cup canned mild green chile peppers, chopped and drained

In a large heavy skillet, sauté spinach in olive oil over moderate heat *just* until tender, but not soft and mushy. Set aside; allow to cool. Preheat another cast-iron skillet; *do not allow skillet to smoke.* Spread tortillas with cream cheese; dividing evenly. Spread spinach over cream cheese, dividing evenly. Spinkle each with chiles; evenly fold in half and grill untill each tortilla starts to crisp, turning constantly.

SOPAS
y
ESTOFADOS

Albóndigas
(Classic Meat Ball Soup)
8 servings

2 eggs, beaten
1 pound lean ground beef
1 cup cooked rice
1 tablespoon chili powder
1 1/2 teaspoons minced *fresh* cilantro
1 teaspoon minced *fresh* or 1/2 teaspoon dried oregano
1/2 teaspoon minced peeled garlic
Salt and freshly ground black pepper to taste
8 cups beef broth
4 medium firm *ripe* tomatoes, peeled and chopped
2 medium carrots, peeled and chopped
2 medium green bell peppers, cored, seeded, and chopped
1 medium onion, peeled and chopped
Water as needed

In a medium bowl, combine eggs, beef, rice, chili powder, cilantro, oregano, garlic, and salt and pepper to taste, mixing well. Form meat mixture into small balls, *each* about 1/2 inch in diameter. Heat beef broth in a large heavy saucepan or stockpot to simmer over moderate heat. Add meat balls to broth, a few at a time. Bring broth to a boil; skim foam from surface of soup. Add tomatoes, carrots, peppers, and onions; return broth to a boil. Reduce heat and simmer, uncovered, for 20 minutes. Add salt and pepper to taste. Add water, if necessary, if soup becomes too thick.

Black Bean Soup
8 servings

1 pound dried black beans
Water as needed
3 garlic cloves, peeled and minced
1 medium onion, peeled and chopped
2 tablespoons hot *extra virgin* olive oil
1 bay leaf
1 tablespoon minced green bell pepper
1 1/2 teaspoons salt or to taste
1/2 teaspoon ground cumin
1 tablespoon minced *fresh* cilantro for garnish

Spread beans over a flat surface; remove any foreign particles. Rinse beans in cold water; drain thoroughly, rinse again, and drain again thoroughly. In a large heavy saucepan, sauté onions and garlic in olive oil over moderate heat, stirring constantly, until onion is tender but not soft. Add 6 cups water, beans, bay leaf, green pepper, salt, and cumin. Bring to a boil over high heat; reduce temperature and simmer, cover ajar, for 3 hours. Sprinkle cilantro over soup *just* before serving.

Chilpotle Pepper Chicken Soup
8 to 10 servings

I prepare a variation of the same soup by adding 2 cups cooked rice or egg noodles.

2 garlic cloves, peeled and minced
2 cups chopped celery
2 cups chopped peeled onion
1 cup chopped peeled carrot
2 tablespoons hot *extra virgin* olive oil
1 1/2 pounds boneless chicken breast, skin removed and cut into thin
   strips
8 cups water
1 ounce or 2 tablespoons minced *fresh* chilpotle chile peppers
1 tablespoon salt or to taste
1 tablespoon minced *fresh* cilantro
1 *ripe* avocado, peeled, seeded, sliced, and immediately
   sprinkled with *fresh* lime juice (see note)

In a large heavy stockpot, sauté garlic, celery, onion, and carrot in olive oil over moderate heat until tender but not soft. Add chicken strips and brown quickly. Add water, peppers, and salt; bring to a boil over high heat. Reduce temperature and simmer, cover ajar, for 10 minutes. Add cilantro *just* before serving. Garnish *each* serving with avocado slices.

Note: Preferably use the bumpy skinned California Haas avocado.

Charro Bean Sopa
(Cowboy Bean Soup)
6 to 8 servings

By adding a few fresh ingredients here and there, freshly cooked pinto beans have many wonderful uses. Try this recipe some cold winter night accompanied with freshly-made flour tortillas and steaming Mexican hot chocolate.

4 to 6 cups cooked Charro Beans (include bean liquid) (see index)
1 jalapeño chile pepper, cut into thin strips
2 cups chopped firm *ripe* tomato
1/2 cup chopped peeled onion
2 tablespoons minced *fresh* or 1 tablespoon dried cilantro
Hot water as needed
Additional minced *fresh* cilantro for garnish

In a large heavy saucepan or medium heavy stockpot, combine the first 6 ingredients. Bring to a boil over moderate heat; reduce temperature slightly and simmer briskly for 30 minutes. Add water as necessary so that beans do not become too thick or dry. Ladle hot soup into bowls and garnish each serving with additional minced *fresh* cilantro. Bean mixture may be strained, draining off some of the liquid, and served as a side dish, if desired.

Chili Verde
(Green Chili)
about 6 servings

*Chili Verde is one of the staples of all New Mexican households and restaurants —
a dish varied in methods and styles from one person to the next. It is similar to
having a favorite secret family spaghetti recipe.*

1 pound New Mexico or Anaheim mild chile peppers, roasted and
    peeled, and cut into thin strips
About 3 (2-ounce) jalapeño chile peppers, roasted, peeled and
    minced (see directions, page 73)
2 pounds boneless pork shoulder (butt), cut into 3/4 to 1-inch cubes
1/4 cup hot cooking oil
1 garlic clove, peeled and minced
4 cups water
2 cups chopped peeled firm *ripe* tomatoes or 1 (15-ounce) can
    Italian-style plum tomatoes
1 teaspoon minced *fresh* or 1/2 teaspoon dried Mexican oregano
1/2 teaspoon ground cumin
1 cup flour
1 cup cold water
Salt and freshly ground black pepper to taste

Prepare peppers and set aside. In a Dutch oven or large heavy saucepan,
thoroughly brown pork in oil over moderate heat; do not drain. Add peppers, garlic, 4 cups water, tomatoes, oregano, and cumin, mixing well;
bring mixture to a boil. In a 2-cup measure, gradually blend cold water
into the flour. (If the mixture is lumpy, pour mixture through a sieve or
strainer, breaking the flour particles or lumps with a wooden spoon.)
Quickly blend mixture into the chili; reduce heat and simmer, uncovered,
for 10 to 15 minutes. Serve as desired.

Chimayo Corn Chowder
8 to 10 servings

*Chimayo is about 25 miles north of Santa Fe, New Mexico. The Chimayo chile pep-
per is renowned for being used to make the best ground New Mexico-style chili
powder. Although there are three different types of peppers in this soup, the
Chimayo is the one that gives it its spunk or spice.*

6 pounds freshly cut whole-kernel corn or 6 (16-ounce) cans
    drained whole-kernel or cream-style canned corn
1/4 cup *extra virgin* olive oil
1/2 cup minced peeled onion
1/2 cup chopped *fresh* Anaheim mild green chile peppers
1/2 cup chopped sweet red bell pepper
1/4 cup minced *fresh* Chimayo chile peppers or 2 tablespoons
    New Mexico-style (bright red) chili powder
1 tablespoon salt or to taste

1 teaspoon white pepper or to taste
1 teaspoon ground cumin
6 tablespoons corn starch
3 cups cold water

If using whole-kernel corn, process or blend in a food processor or blender until corn is almost a pureé. In a large heavy saucepan or stockpot, heat oil over moderate heat. Add onion and sauté until tender but not browned. Add corn, peppers, and seasonings. Bring to a slow boil, about 20 minutes. In a 4-cup measure, blend cold water into the corn starch, blending until mixture is smooth. Stir corn starch mixture into the corn mixture. *Be careful not to scorch mixture.* Reduce heat and continue to simmer for 5 minutes. Serve *very* hot.

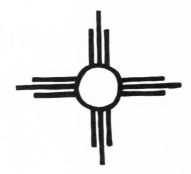

Gazpacho
(Chilled Crisp Raw Vegetable Soup)
8 servings

2 medium firm *ripe* tomatoes, chopped
1 medium cucumber, peeled, seeded, and minced
1 small sweet red bell pepper, cored, seeded, and chopped
1 small green bell pepper, cored, seeded, and chopped
1/2 medium onion, peeled and minced
4 cups canned tomato juice
2 tablespoons red wine vinegar
2 tablespoons *extra virgin* olive oil
2 tablespoons *fresh* lime juice
1 teaspoon minced *fresh* jalapeño chile pepper
1 tablespoon minced *fresh* or 1/2 teaspoon dried oregano
2 tablespoons minced *fresh* cilantro, divided, for garnish
8 thin lime wedges, divided, for garnish

Combine all ingredients together in a large bowl, except cilantro and lime. Cover and chill for several hours in the refrigerator; serve cold. Ladle into soup bowls and garnish *each* with minced cilantro and a wedge of lime.

Posole
(Hominy Soup)
8 to 10 servings

Posole is a New Mexican dish that's rich and hearty. Many different meats or even fish can be used in place of pork. One of my other favorites is chicken. Use the little drumettes. To add spice, accompany Posole with Salsa Verde or guijillo chile peppers.

6 slices bacon
1 pound lean ground pork
2 garlic cloves, peeled and minced
1 small onion, peeled and chopped
2 teaspoons minced *fresh* or 1 teaspoon dried oregano
1 teaspoon salt or to taste
1/4 teaspoon ground cumin
6 ounces Anaheim mild green chile peppers, *fresh* or canned
2 pounds or 2 (29-ounce) cans posole (see note)
8 cups water
Salsa Verde (see index) or guijillo chile peppers to taste (see note)

In a large heavy stockpot, pan-fry bacon over moderate heat until crisp. Remove bacon, drain well, crumble, and set aside; drain off and discard drippings. Add pork to stockpot and lightly brown pork, breaking it up as it cooks. Add garlic, onion, oregano, salt, and cumin to stockpot Drain off about three fourths of the fat. Add bacon and remaining ingredients; reduce heat and simmer, cover ajar, for 15 to 20 minutes. Serve in soup bowls accompanied with Salsa Verde or guijillo chile peppers.

Note: Posole is white hominy, available fresh in specialty stores in Mexico and the southwest U.S.A. In other areas of the U.S., it is available in 8, 16, and 32-ounce cans.

Note: These mild chile peppers are available in a powdered dried form in specialty food stores.

Menudo
(Tripe Soup)
8 large servings

Menudo is said to have healing powers. This is one of my oldest family recipes. Its rich taste and aroma are indisputable.

4 pounds honey comb tripe (see note)
4 garlic cloves, peeled and minced
2 cups chopped peeled onions
Water as needed
1 teaspoon minced fresh or 1/2 teaspoon dried oregano
1/2 teaspoon ground cumin
2 (16-ounce) cans hominy
1/2 cup (3 ounces) New Mexico-style (bright red) chili powder

2 tablespoons ancho-style (dark) chili powder
1 tablespoon salt or to taste
1 cup chopped peeled onion for garnish, divided
1/2 cup minced *fresh* cilantro for garnish, divided
1/2 cup minced *fresh* or 1/4 cup dried oregano for garnish, divided
8 lemon wedges for garnish, divided
Warm corn or flour tortillas

Cut tripe into bite-size strips and place in an 8-quart heavy stockpot. Add garlic, 16 cups (4 quarts) water, onion, oregano, and cumin. Bring to a boil over high heat; reduce temperature and simmer, cover ajar, for 4 hours until tripe is tender. Skim foam from the surface. Rinse tripe in cold water quickly. Return to heat; add hominy, chili powder, and water to cover. Bring mixture to a boil over moderate heat. Serve very hot. Pass remaining onion, cilantro, oregano, and lemon wedges as garnishes. Serve with corn or flour tortillas, as desired.

Note: Tripe is the lining of a steer's stomach. It is available in the meat section of most grocery stores. It may need to be ordered in advance.

Lista's Chili with Beans
6 to 8 servings

Quick and easy to prepare. Garnish with cheese and jalapeños for extra color and spice.

2 pounds *lean* ground beef
1 large onion, peeled and chopped
1 medium green bell pepper, cored, seeded, and chopped
3 firm *ripe* large tomatoes, peeled and diced
1/4 cup chopped pickled jalapeño chile pepper
1 (46-ounce) can tomato juice
3/4 cup New Mexico-style (bright red) chili powder
1 tablespoon crushed dried hot red pepper
1 1/2 teaspoons granulated dried garlic or 1 to 2 garlic cloves,
    peeled and minced
1 1/2 tablespoons freshly ground black pepper
2 teaspoons dried oregano
6 cups cooked pinto or red kidney beans, drained
Shredded Monterey Jack or Co-Jack cheese and whole jalapeño
    chile peppers for garnish

In a large heavy saucepan, brown ground beef over moderate heat; drain thoroughly. Add onion and continue cooking until onion is *just* tender but not soft. Add remaining ingredients, except beans and garnishes. Bring mixture to a boil. Reduce heat and simmer, partially covered, over low heat for 30 minutes. Add beans; continue to simmer for 5 to 10 minutes. Ladle into large soup bowls and garnish with shredded cheese and jalapeño chile peppers.

Caldo de Res
(Beef Shank Soup)
4 servings

Ask your butcher to cut a beef shank into about 1 1/2-inch slices. In order for this recipe to work correctly and look right, each serving must have its own beef shank.

1/2 cup flour
Salt as needed
1 teaspoon freshly ground black pepper or to taste
1 teaspoon granulated dried garlic or 1 to 2 garlic cloves, peeled and
    minced
4 (6 to 8-ounce) beef shank slices (see note)
4 cups very coarsely chopped green cabbage
3 large potatoes, peeled and cut into very large pieces
3 tomatoes, peeled and cut into wedges
2 cups water
2 bay leaves
1 tablespoon minced *fresh* or 1 1/2 teaspoons dried oregano
2 garlic cloves, peeled and minced
1 cup *very* coarsely cut peeled carrots, cut into 1-inch pieces
1 cup *very* coarsely chopped peeled onion
1 cup *very* coarsely chopped green bell peppers
1 cup *very* coarsely chopped celery
Hot cooked rice
Soft tortillas or Bolillos (see index) warmed in a preheated *very*
    slow oven (250°F.)

In a large bowl, combine flour, 1 teaspoon salt, pepper, and granulated garlic. Dip beef shanks into flour mixture, coating *each* lightly. Shake *each* shank to remove excess flour mixture. In a large heavy skillet, brown shanks thoroughly, all sides, about 8 to 10 minutes. Drain off excess drippings; set aside. In a large heavy stockpot, combine vegetables, water, chili powder, minced *fresh* garlic, oregano, and salt to taste. Cook for 30 minutes. Add meat and continue to cook for an additional 20 to 30 minutes. Serve in large bowls with rice, one shank piece per serving. Accompany with warm tortillas or Bolillos for sopping up the broth.

Note: Have butcher cut a whole beef shank into individual slices.

Chili Colorado
6 to 8 servings

Many people are familiar with Carne Guisada from the Texas and (old) Mexico areas. Similar to a beef stew, but with a kick! — its flavor and color are much richer due to the addition of the beautiful potent red chiles grown in New Mexico. Of course, warm tortillas help to sop up the wonderful gravy!

2 pounds beef tenderloin or boneless sirloin or chuck or round
    steak, cut into 1-inch pieces
1/4 cup hot cooking oil

1 garlic clove, peeled and minced
1 cup flour
3/4 cup New Mexico-style (bright red) chili powder
3 cups beef broth (see note)
1/2 teaspoon ground cumin
Frijóles Refritos (refried beans) (see index)
Warm flour or corn tortillas or French bread as desired

In a large heavy skillet, brown the beef thoroughly in oil over moderate heat, stirring frequently. Add the garlic while the beef is browning. Remove beef, draining well, and set aside. Add flour to pan and brown lightly over moderate heat, stirring constantly. Add chili powder, mixing well. Gradually add broth, blending quickly with a wire whisk so that lumps do not form. Add beef and cumin, mixing well. Reduce heat and simmer for 30 minutes. Serve hot accompanied with Frijóles Refritos and warm flour or corn tortillas or French bread.

Chili (the stew) Styles:

Chile or Chili — *There is much argument in the United States as to the proper use of chile versus chili. In this book, we refer to chile for the various types of peppers and the recipes prepared with them. Chili is used to designate the stew-like recipe which has become an American institution with infinite recipes and nuances.*

Colorado/New Mexico/Arizona:
Chili is green here. Made with fresh green chiles much like authentic Hopi and Navajo stews. Usually pork, but lamb or even venison is the meat of choice used in hefty chunks.

California:
Brightly colored chili, lighter, and leaner than other versions but typical of California. Sometimes vegetarian, sometimes with chicken, but always with a lot of vegetables. Garnish also is plentiful (sour cream, cheese, lettuce, black olives, even bean sprouts).

American:
A rich full-bodied stew consisting of ground beef with lots of tomatoes, beans, cumin, oregano, garlic, and onion. Thickness varies with each cook; spiciness varies with the region.

Texas Trail Chili:
This style is typically made without tomatoes or beans — one for the Purists. It is prepared with a tougher cut of beef cooked with hot peppers, but options such as onions, garlic, cumin, and oregano now days are acceptable. The meat can be ground, but the authentic version is hand-diced.

Chicago/Cincinnati:
This version is thin, mild, and slightly sweet. It reflects the eastern European influence of some of the settlers. The spicing is subtle.

Ernesto's Vegetable Beef Soup

10 to 12 servings
(Just a few of our family members!)

To an Evangelista, cooking soups and stews just comes naturally, which probably has something to do with Dad. Recently my brother Ernesto and I were reminiscing about him and his cooking. We remember looking around the family kitchen and in the refrigerator to see if we could guess the contents of the evening meal.

When Florencio P. Evangelista would go into the kitchen, you'd hear the familar clack clack of the knife hitting the cutting board, and clang of a pot or pan. Magically there would be the aroma of bay leaf or ginger root or garlic along with the sizzle of meat searing. Seconds would pass before curiosity and a warm feeling would overcome us. We knew a culinary treat was in store for us.

Now, when Ernie cooks some of Dad's recipes, that same warm feeling happens to me again. We at Lista's hope the recipes of this book will cultivate similar memories of childhood for you.

Serve Ernesto's soup with hot Jalapeño Corn Bread as a cold winter evening specialty.

2 to 2 1/2 pounds boneless beef chuck, rump, top round, or other
    stewing beef
2 tablespoons hot cooking oil
1 medium onion, peeled and cut into medium wedges
1 garlic clove, peeled and chopped
2 beef bouillon cubes
2 bay leaves
16 cups (4 quarts) hot water, divided
1 teaspoon freshly ground black pepper or to taste
1/4 teaspoon ground cloves
4 medium potatoes, peeled and cubed or cut into medium pieces
2 large carrots, peeled and cubed or cut into medium pieces
1 pound green cabbage, cored and cut into thin wedges, or coarsely
    chopped or shredded
2 cups sliced zucchini squash
Salt to taste
Jalapeño Corn Bread (see index)

With a sharp knife, trim off all fat from beef; cut meat into 3/4 to 1-inch cubes. In a large heavy stockpot, thoroughly brown beef in oil over moderate heat. Add onion and garlic; sauté *just* until tender. Add boullion cubes, bay leaves, 3 cups water, pepper, and cloves. Simmer, partially covered, for 20 to 30 minutes; add remaining water, potatoes, and carrots. Bring mixture to a brisk simmer; continue to simmer, partially covered, until meat is fork tender, about 30 minutes. Reduce heat, add cabbage and squash and continue to simmer, stirring occasionally, until cabbage is tender but not mushy, about 8 to 10 minutes. Add salt to taste and adjust other seasonings, if desired. Serve with hot Jalapeño Corn Bread.

Atún con Broccoli
(Tuna Steaks with Broccoli)
4 servings

The key to the preparation of this recipe is to have the tuna, broccoli, and sauce ready to serve at the same time so all are served at the correct temperature.

2 cups Salsa Blanca (New Mexican Jalapeño Cream Sauce)(see page 51)
2 pounds *fresh* broccoli or 2 (10-ounce) packages frozen broccoli spears
About 4 cups water
4 *fresh* jalapeño chile peppers, seeds removed
2 garlic cloves
1/4 cup *extra virgin* olive oil
4 (8 to 10-ounce) *fresh* or frozen tuna steaks (see note)
Lemon wedges as desired for garnish

Prepare Salsa Blanca; cover and set aside. Clean *fresh* broccoli, separating into spears, and removing any woody stems. In a large heavy saucepan or small heavy stockpot, bring water (about 2 inches in depth) to a brisk boil over high heat. Add broccoli, jalapeño chile peppers, and garlic; cook, uncovered, 10 to 15 minutes for *fresh* broccoli or until *just* tender, and according to package directions for frozen broccoli. Drain well; keep warm. *Do not overcook broccoli.*

While broccoli is cooking, reheat Salsa Blanca; keep warm. Heat olive oil to medium (350°F.) in a large heavy cast-iron or other skillet. Add tuna steaks and pan-fry *each* for 2 minutes per side. Arrange tuna steaks and broccoli spears on individual plates, dividing evenly. Spoon Salsa Blanca over *each* tuna steak and garnish with lemon wedges.

Note: Preferably use fresh tuna. If frozen is used, thaw completely before pan-frying.

Arroz con Camarón
(Shrimp with Rice)
4 servings

20 jumbo *(16 to 20 count)* shrimp, peeled, deveined, and tails
   removed
4 garlic cloves, peeled and minced
2 large sweet red bell peppers, cored, seeded, and cut into thin long strips
1 large yellow onion, peeled and cut into thin long strips
4 tablespoons hot *extra virgin* olive oil
1 teaspoon minced *fresh* or 1/2 teaspoon dried Mexican oregano
1/2 teaspoon crushed dried hot red pepper
1/4 teaspoon ground cumin
Hot cooked rice as desired
1 tablespoon minced *fresh* cilantro for garnish, divided
Thin lemon wedges for garnish

Prepare shrimp for cooking; set aside. In a large heavy skillet, sauté garlic, sweet red pepper, and onion in olive oil over moderate heat until tender but crisp. Add shrimp, oregano, dried red pepper, and cumin to skillet, stirring constantly; continue to sauté for 2 to 3 minutes, *just* until shrimp become opaque and turn coral pink in color. Lay a bed of rice on *each* dinner plate; arrange shrimp and sweet red bell pepper and onion strips atop the rice, dividing evenly. Spoon remaining pan drippings over *each* serving and garnish with minced cilantro and thin lemon wedges.

Barbecued Chicken Tacos
(Stuffed Folded Soft Flour Tortilla)
4 servings

I like any tacos hotly spiced, so this recipe calls for Lista's Aduvada Sauce or other hot-spiced barbecue sauce. You may wish to substitute Lista's Aduvada Sauce with a sweeter, more mildly spiced sauce.

1/4 cup minced green bell pepper
1/4 cup minced peeled onion
1 tablespoon hot *extra virgin* olive oil
8 ounces (about 2 cups) cut-up cooked chicken,
1/2 cup Aduvada Sauce (see index) or barbecue sauce of choice
8 flour tortillas
2 cups shredded iceberg lettuce, divided
1 cup shredded Monterey Jack or sharp Cheddar cheese, divided
1/2 cup chopped firm *ripe* tomato, divided
Frijóles Refritos (refried beans) (see index) or cooked black beans
Spanish Rice (see index)
2 cups Lista's Hot Sauce for garnish (see index)

In a medium heavy skillet, sauté pepper and onion in olive oil over moderate heat until *just* tender. Add chicken and barbecue sauce, mixing well. Reduce heat and simmer for 3 to 5 minutes. Warm tortillas on a baking sheet in a preheated very slow oven (250°F.) for 3 to 4 minutes, being sure tortillas remain soft. Spoon chicken taco filling into *each* warm tortilla, dividing evenly. Layer lettuce, cheese, and tomato onto *each*. Fold over *each* tortilla and arrange on individual plates, two per serving. Spoon Frijóles Refritos or black beans and Spanish Rice next to the tacos. Pass Lista's Hot Sauce in a sauceboat as a garnish.

Beef Enchiladas New Mexico-style
4 servings

These are Lista's most popular enchiladas. We call them Old-Fashioned Stacked Enchiladas, which are stacked rather than rolled, as is the style in New Mexico. Choose your filling and enjoy.

Enchilada Sauce

1 cup flour
1/2 cup New Mexico-style (bright red) chili powder
1/2 teaspoon garlic powder
1/2 teaspoon ground cumin
About 3 cups warm water, divided
Salt to taste

About 1 cup cooking oil
12 corn tortillas
2 cups Meat Filling for Tacos, Enchiladas, or Burritos (see index)
1/4 cup chopped peeled onion
2 cups shredded Monterey Jack or sharp Cheddar, Colby, or
   Queso Anjo cheese
3 cups shredded iceberg lettuce
1 cup chopped firm *ripe* tomatoes
Frijóles Refritos (refried beans) (optional) (see index)
Spanish Rice (optional) (see index)

To prepare sauce, brown the flour in a medium heavy cast-iron or other skillet over moderate heat until flour turns a light brown in color. Add garlic powder and cumin, mixing well. Gradually add water, 1/2 cup at a time, blending well to dissolve any flour lumps. Add salt. Reduce heat to very low and simmer, uncovered, for 10 to 15 minutes; set aside.

To pan-fry tortillas, heat oil in a shallow medium skillet to medium high (350 to 375°F.). *Do not allow oil to smoke.* Carefully pan-fry tortillas, one at a time, until tortillas are warmed but remain soft and pliable. *Do not allow tortillas to become crisp.* Drain *each* well on absorbent paper.

Dip 4 tortillas at a time in prepared sauce, then arrange on a large ungreased baking sheet. Top *each* with about 2 tablespoons of meating filling, 1 teaspoon onion, and 1 tablespoon cheese. Repeat process of dipping tortillas; top *each* filled tortilla on the baking sheet with a second dipped tortilla. Repeat complete process, ending with meat filling, onion, and cheese atop *each* tortilla stack. Bake in a preheated *very* slow oven (275°F.) for 5 to 8 minutes or until cheese is melted. Using a large metal spatula, transfer *each* tortilla stack to an individual plate. Garnish *each* serving with shredded lettuce and chopped tomato and accompany with Frijóles Refritos and Spanish Rice, if desired.

Beef Tenderloin with
Black Bean and Green Chile Salsa
4 servings

Black Bean and Green Chile Salsa is one of Lista's most versatile sauces and may be served with beef tenderloin, swordfish, pork tenderloin, or chicken breasts. My favorite vegetable to serve with grilled beef filets is Calabacitas. I'm sure you'll find your favorite.

4 (7-ounce) beef filets (tenderloin)
4 corn tortillas, crisp-fried, or crisp tostada shells
2 cups Black Bean and Green Chile Salsa or as desired, divided (see index) 4 corn tortillas, cut into strips, crisp-fried, and lightly salted, for garnish, divided

Arrange filets on the grill rack of a charcoal grill, 8 to 10 inches above medium coals, (ash gray and glowing) in a charcoal grill fire box. Grill about 10 to 14 minutes total, about 4 to 6 minutes per side for medium rare to medium. Or, arrange filets on a rack in a broiler pan. Broil, 4 to 6 inches from heat source, until desired degree of doneness, about 4 to 5 minutes per side for medium rare to medium. Or, sauté filets in a hot lightly greased large heavy skillet over high heat, about 1 1/2 minutes per side.

Place a tostada shell on *each* dinner plate; arrange a grilled filet in the center of *each*. Spoon about 1/2 cup of salsa over *each* steak. Sprinkle *each* with crisp tortilla strips.

Note: Doneness of filets may also be determined by the touch test. With the forefinger, press each filet lightly. Rare filets will be very soft to the touch; medium rare, soft to firm to the touch; medium, springy firm to the touch, and well done, hard (forget it!) When the filets are cut, the interior will be blood red for rare, red to pink for medium rare, light pink, no juices running for medium, and gray (sad!) for well-done.

Burgers Galore
one serving

7 ounces ground beef (top round or sirloin)
1 Kaiser roll, split in half and buttered
Crisp leaf lettuce as desired
2 slices firm *ripe* tomato
3 to 4 dill pickle slices
1 thin slice peeled red onion, separated into rings
Variety of condiments of choice

Shape beef into 4-inch diameter patty. Grill, broil, charcoal-grill, or pan-fry beef patty to desired degree of doneness, abut 3 minutes per side for medium rare. *Do not overcook.* See Beef Tenderloin with Black Bean and Green Chile Salsa for specific charcoal grilling and broiling instructions (page 39). Grill or broil cut surfaces of Kaiser roll until lightly toasted. Arrange grilled beef patty on bottom half of the roll. Garnish with lettuce, tomato slices, pickle slices, and onion rings. Top with remaining roll half. Serve immediately. Pass condiments of choice.

Variations:

Lista's Burger - Add 6 pickled jalapeño chile pepper slices (hot) or a grilled opened whole Ortega pepper (mild) (see note). Sprinkle 1/2 cup shredded Monterey Jack cheese over beef patty on bun. Grill or broil until cheese is melted, about 2 to 3 minutes. Top with remaining listed ingredients.

Note: To grill pepper, see page 73

Bacon Cheeseburger - Sprinkle beef patty with 1/2 cup shredded cheese of choice. Melt cheese as previously directed. Top with 3 crisp-cooked bacon slices and remaining previously listed ingredients.

Colorado Burger - Combine 2 tablespoons Charro Beans (see index), 2 tablespoons Chili Colorado (see index) and 2 tablespoons Meat Filling for Tacos, Enchiladas, or Burritos (see index); spread over cooked beef burger on roll. Top with 1/3 cup shredded Monterey Jack cheese and 2 tablespoons chopped peeled onion.

Mexican Burger - Shape ground beef into an oval shape before grilling. Place cooked burger in a thin burrito-style tortilla. Top in order with 1/3 cup Frijóles Refritos (see index) 2 to 4 tablespoons Chili Verde (see index). Fold sides of tortilla inward, overlapping one over the other. Garnish with shredded iceberg lettuce, chopped tomato, and shredded Monterey Jack or sharp Cheddar cheese.

Carne Aduvada
(Pork in Aduvada Sauce)
4 to 6 servings

Carne Aduvada is a marvelous pork dish flavored with oregano, cumin, garlic, and chile caribe; however, it does require some advance preparation. The meat must marinate in the marinade for at least twenty four hours. This recipe is equally good prepared with boneless chicken breasts.

2 beef bouillon cubes, mashed
1 (15-ounce) can tomato sauce or 2 cups prepared tomato sauce,
  recipe of choice
1 cup chile caribe
1/4 cup sugar
1 tablespoon granulated dried garlic or 3 to 4 garlic cloves,
  peeled and minced
2 teaspoons minced *fresh* or 1 teaspoon dried oregano
1 1/2 teaspoons salt or to taste
1/4 teaspoon ground cumin
2 pounds pork tenderloin or boneless pork shoulder (butt), thinly sliced
Papas de la Casa (see index)
Cooked *fresh* vegetable of choice
Flour tortillas as desired warmed in a preheated very slow oven (250°F.)

In a large bowl, combine the first 8 ingredients, mixing well with a wire whisk. Add pork slices, coating *each* well. Cover and refrigerate for 24 hours. Transfer mixture to a 2-quart baking dish. Bake, covered, in a preheated slow oven (325°F.) for 1 1/2 hours. Serve with Papas de la Casa, *fresh* vegetables of choice, and warmed tortillas.

> *Chile caribe is a mild to medium-spiced crushed dried pepper available in many specialty grocery stores.*

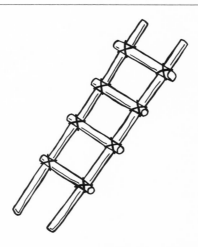

Carne Asada
(Roasted Meat)
6 servings

Asada means roasted in Spanish. Each cook has his or her own interpretation of the meaning and a recipe to go with it.

1/2 cup *extra virgin* olive oil
1/3 cup red wine vinegar
2 tablespoons minced *fresh* or 1 tablespoon dried cilantro
2 tablespoons minced *fresh* or 1 tablespoon dried oregano
1 tablespoon freshly ground black pepper or to taste
1 1/2 teaspoons chile caribe or crushed dried hot red pepper
3 pounds beef skirt or sirloin steak, cut 1/4 to 1/2-inch thick
Flour or corn tortillas as desired
Salsa Fresca, or Pico de Gallo, or Avocado Relish (see index)

In a large bowl, combine the first 6 ingredients, blending well. Add meat, coating *each* piece well with the marinade; cover and refrigerate for at least 4 hours. Remove steak pieces from marinade, draining well. Arrange steaks on a grill rack, 8 to 10 inches above medium coals (ash gray and glowing), in a charcoal grill fire box; grill about 4 to 5 minutes per side for medium rare or to desired degree of doneness. With a sharp knife, cut across the grain into 6 serving pieces, *each* about 8 ounces. While steaks are grilling, arrange tortillas on a baking sheet; warm in a very slow oven (250°F.) for about 5 minutes, with tortillas retaining their softness. Accompany *each* serving with warmed tortillas and salsa or relish of choice.

Carne Cangrejo
(Beef and Crab)
6 servings

The combination of fine beef and fresh lump crabmeat is one of our house favorites. We finish this specialty with Lista's New Mexican Jalapeño Cream Sauce. This dish is very rich. We accompany it with a small amount of trimmings or vegetables. Our customers' favorites have been white rice with black beans.

1 pound lump crabmeat (see note)
Salsa Blanca (New Mexican Jalapeño Cream Sauce) (see index)
6 (10 to 12 ounce) beef rib-eye or Delmonico steaks

Prepare jalapeño cream sauce and keep warm in the top of a double boiler over hot water or in an electric crock pot set at the low setting. Arrange filets on the grill rack of a charcoal grill, 8 to 10 inches above medium coals, (ash gray and glowing) in a charcoal grill fire box. Grill about 8 to 14 minutes total, about 4 to 7 minutes per side for medium rare to medium. Or, arrange filets on a rack in a broiler pan. Broil, 4 to 6 inches from heat source, to desired degree of doneness, about 4 to 5 minutes per side for medium rare to medium. Or, sauté filets in a hot lightly greased large heavy skillet over high heat, about 2 minutes per side. Spoon warmed crab-meat atop *each* steak, dividing evenly. Ladle about 1/2 to 3/4 cup cream sauce over *each* steak. Serve immediately.

Note: Pick over crabmeat, removing any shell or cartilage. Heat slightly in a small heavy saucepan over low heat, stirring gently, but being careful not to break up crabmeat. Cover and keep warm over hot water while preparing steak.

Note: Doneness of filets may also be determined by the touch test (see page 39).

Carnitas Enchiladas
(Enchiladas with Meat)
6 servings

These enchiladas originated as a complement to Lista's popular Chili Verde (green chili), which is very different from any other chili. Eating Carnitas Enchiladas is a quick flavor-trip to northern New Mexico.

2 pounds Carnitas (see index)
3 cups Chili Verde (see index)
12 corn tortillas
1 1/2 cups shredded Monterey Jack cheese
2 to 3 cups Posole, divided (see index)
1 *ripe* medium avocado, peeled, pitted, thinly sliced, and
  immediately sprinkled with lemon juice

Prepare Carnitas, Chili Verde, and Posole in advance. In a large heavy skil-let sprayed with non-stick vegetable oil cooking spray, lightly pan-fry tor-tillas over moderate heat until warm but still soft. *Do not allow tortillas to become crisp.*

Spoon about 2 1/2 ounces (1/4 to 1/3 cup) chopped or shredded Carnitas onto *each* tortilla. Liberally cover Carnitas on *each* with Chili Verde. Top *each* with 2 tablespoons shredded cheese. Garnish *each* serving with 1/3 to 1/2 cup Posole and thin avocado slices.

Twenty-five years ago New Mexican food had a fairly disreputable reputa-tion as dinner chow: cheap, filling, and crude.

Carnitas
(Little Meats)
10 to 12 servings

Preparation of Carnitas may take time but involves little work. The meat is so tender it can easily be shredded or cut into chunks and used as a filling for tacos. It is also one of my favorite fillings for enchiladas accompanied by Salsa Verde.

5 pounds lean pork shoulder (butt)
2 tablespoons minced *fresh* or 1 tablespoon dried oregano
1 tablespoon salt or to taste
1 tablespoon minced *fresh* or 1 1/2 teaspoons dried cilantro
2 teaspoons freshly ground black pepper
1 teaspoon ground cumin
2 large carrots, peeled and chopped
2 medium onions, peeled and chopped
Water as needed
Frijóles Refritos (refried beans) as desired (see index)
Spanish Rice as desired (see index)
Avocado Relish as desired (see index)
Corn tortillas, warmed in a preheated very slow oven (250°F.)

In a Dutch oven or medium heavy stockpot, combine the first 8 ingredients; add enough water to cover. Bring to a boil over moderate heat; reduce temperature and simmer, covered, for 1 1/2 hours. Remove pork, draining well; transfer meat to a 2-quart baking dish. Bake, uncovered, in a preheated slow oven (325°F.) for 1 hour. Drain off any fat. With a fork or sharp knife, shred or chop meat. Serve Carnitas with Frijóles Refritos, Spanish Rice, Avocado Relish, and warmed corn tortillas, if desired.

Chicken Burritos
(Stuffed Soft Flour Tortillas)
4 servings

Literally translated little burro, the following is more of an instruction for preparing burritos than a recipe. Once you've cooked the filling and chili, you need only build the burritos, using a good foundation. Good flour tortillas can be found in most grocery and food specialty stores these days.

2 cups hot water
1 tablespoon minced *fresh* or 1 1/2 teaspoons dried cilantro
2 teaspoons minced *fresh* or 1 teaspoon dried oregano
2 teaspoons New Mexico-style (bright red) chili powder
2 teaspoons salt or to taste
1 teaspoon celery salt
1/2 teaspoon ground cumin
1/2 teaspoon white pepper
2 pounds boneless chicken breasts, skin removed and cut into thin strips
8 corn or flour tortillas, warmed in a preheated very slow oven (250°F.)

Chili Verde (see index) or other favorite prepared chili
Shredded Monterey Jack, sharp Cheddar, or Co-Jack cheese for garnish
Shredded iceberg lettuce and chopped *ripe* tomato for garnish
Spanish Rice (see index) or other favorite rice recipe

In a large heavy saucepan or small Dutch oven, combine water, herbs, and spices; bring to a brisk boil over high heat. Add chicken, being sure pieces are separated, and return mixture to a boil. Remove from heat, cover, and allow to stand for 10 minutes (see note). Drain well. Divide hot chicken onto *each* warm tortilla; roll tortillas, jelly roll-style. Place filled tortillas, 2 per serving, seam-side down on individual plates. Liberally spoon Chili Verde or other desired chili over the tortillas. Sprinkle cheese, as desired, over *each* serving and garnish *each* with shredded iceberg lettuce and chopped tomato. Accompany with Spanish Rice or other desired prepared rice recipe.

Note: Chicken may be used immediately or stored, tightly covered, in the refrigerator for up to 3 days.

Chicken Vera Cruz-Style
2 servings

Salsa Ranchera is one of the most versatile sauces included in this book. Try it with a variety of meats.

1/4 cup *extra virgin* olive oil
2 garlic cloves, peeled and minced
2 (7 to 8-ounce) boneless chicken breasts, skin removed
3 to 4 cups Salsa Ranchera (see index)
1/4 cup dry white wine
2 tablespoons thinly sliced pitted black olives, for garnish
2 tablespoons thinly sliced pitted green olives, for garnish
***Fresh* fruit of choice for garnish**
Spanish Rice (optional) (see index)

Heat oil in a medium heavy skillet over moderate heat; add garlic and sauté for about 1 minute. Add chicken and continue sautéing for about 4 minutes, turning chicken pieces constantly. Add Salsa Ranchera and wine, blending well and covering chicken; reduce heat and simmer, covered, for 7 to 10 minutes. Garnish *each* serving with slices of black and green olives and *fresh* fruit. Accompany with Spanish Rice, if desired.

Chicken Fajitas
8 to 10 servings

This recipe will win you many raves when you serve it to guests at an outdoor gathering. The citrus flavors, as well as the honey, seal in a wonderful flavor. And oh — the wonderful aroma one enjoys while the chicken is grilling — enough talking, let's get on with it!!

2 garlic cloves, peeled and minced
1 cup honey
3/4 cup pineapple juice
3/4 cup orange juice
2 tablespoons minced *fresh* or 1 tablespoon dried cilantro
1 tablespoon paprika
1 tablespoon crushed dried hot red pepper or to taste
1 tablespoon freshly ground black pepper or to taste
10 to 20 (4-ounce) boneless chicken breast pieces, skin removed (see note)
2 to 3 large onions, peeled and cut vertically into thin wedges
2 to 3 large green or sweet red bell peppers, cored, seeded, and cut into
  thin strips or 3/4-inch squares
1 to 2 tablespoons hot *extra virgin* olive oil, or butter, or margarine,
  melted
8 to 10 soft flour or corn tortillas, warmed in a preheated very
  slow oven (250°F.)
Shredded iceberg lettuce as desired for garnish
Shredded sharp Cheddar or Monterey Jack cheese as desired for garnish
Lista's Guacamole (see index)
Charro Beans (see index)
Pico de Gallo (see index)

In a deep large glass bowl, combine the first 8 ingredients, blending well with a wire whisk. Or, combine ingredients in a large zip-lock plastic bag; seal and shake vigorously to mix. Add chicken pieces, coating *each* well. Cover or seal and marinate in the refrigerator for 2 to 6 hours. Drain, allowing some of the marinade to remain on the chicken. Arrange chicken pieces on a grill rack, 8 to 10 inches above medium coals (ash gray and glowing), in a charcoal grill fire box. Grill chicken, about 4 to 5 minutes per side, turning pieces frequently with long barbecue tongs. *Do not burn chicken.* For gas grills, follow manufacturer's instructions.

While chicken is grilling, sauté onions and bell peppers in oil in a large heavy skillet over moderate heat until tender but not soft. To serve, cut the grilled chicken pieces across the grain into thin strips. Arrange a warm soft tortilla on *each* dinner plate; top *each* with shredded lettuce, grilled chicken pieces, sautéed vegetables, and cheese, dividing evenly. Accompany *each* serving with Lista's Guacamole and Charro Beans. Pass Pico de Gallo in a sauceboat.

Note: About 3 to 3 1/2 pounds boneless chicken breasts or 2 to 3 whole bone-in chicken breasts will provide the amount of chicken required for this recipe. Boneless chicken breasts will need to be cut into 4 ounce portions while bone-in chicken breasts will need to be skinned, boned, and then cut into portions.

Filet Chilpotle
(Beef Filet with Chilpotle Chile Pepper Sauce)
4 servings

Chilpotle chile peppers are native to New Mexico and to me are the tastiest of the peppers, especially when marinated in an Adobo-style sauce. They usually can be found in the specialty section of grocery stores in 4 to 6-ounce cans. Use them sparingly and with care as they are very hot!

4 cups Chilpotle Pepper Sauce (see index)
4 (6 to 8-ounce) beef filets (tenderloin)
2 cups shredded Monterey Jack cheese, divided
Piñón Spinach (see index)
Charro Beans (see index)

Prepare Chilpotle Pepper Sauce; keep warm over low heat while preparing filets. Grill filets as directed in Beef Tenderloin with Black Bean and Green Chile Salsa (see index). You may wish to undercook the filets slightly before adding cheese so that they do not become overcooked while the cheese is melting. Sprinkle cheese over filets, dividing evenly. Return filets to grill or other heat source, cheese side up, *just* until cheese is melted, about 2 to 3 minutes. Arrange steaks on heated oven-proof dinner plates. Serve immediately accompanied with Piñón Spinach and Charro Beans. Pass the sauce to spoon over *each* filet.

Chilpotle Pepper Veal
(Veal Cutlets with Chilpotle Chile Pepper Sauce)
4 servings

The smoky aroma and taste of these peppers complements the tender veal. This entree is earthy — it tastes like it's good for you. We usually serve Chilpotle Pepper Veal with steamed carrots or green beans.

2 pounds veal cutlet, cut into thin 2-ounce slices
1 cup flour
1 teaspoon garlic powder
1 teaspoon salt or to taste
1 teaspoon white pepper or to taste
1/2 cup butter or margarine, melted
4 cups Chilpotle Pepper Sauce (see index)

Lightly pound veal with a meat mallet. On a sheet of waxed paper, combine flour, garlic powder, salt, and pepper. Dredge *each* veal piece in flour mixture, coating lightly. In a medium heavy skillet, sauté veal in butter over moderate heat, until veal is thoroughly browned, turning occasionally, about 4 to 5 minutes. Sauté 6 pieces at a time; remove sautéed pieces and set aside. *Do not overcook veal as it will become tough.* After all the veal has been sautéed, return veal to skillet; pour Chilpotle Pepper Sauce over veal. Reduce heat and simmer, covered, for 20 minutes, stirring occasionally.

Chorizo
(Spicy Pork Sausage)
about 2 1/2 pounds

2 1/2 pounds lean pork, ground
1 ounce (2 tablespoons) ancho-style (dark) chili powder
1/2 ounce (1 tablespoon) New Mexico-style (bright red) chili powder
1/2 cup red wine vinegar
1 tablespoon cooking oil
1 tablespoon salt or to taste
1 tablespoon crushed dried hot red pepper or crushed dried chile pequin
1 1/2 teaspoons paprika
1 1/2 teaspoons garlic powder
1 1/2 teaspoons minced *fresh* or 3/4 teaspoon dried oregano
1/4 teaspoon ground cloves
1/4 teaspoon ground cumin
1/8 teaspoon cinnamon

In a large bowl, crock, or roasting pan, combine all ingredients, mixing well with the hands, making sure there are no clumps of pork not mixed with the spices. Sausage should be an even, rich red color. Divide sausage mixture into 8 ounce or 1 pound portions. Wrap in heavy-duty aluminum foil, sealing tightly; freeze until firm and store in the freezer for up to 3 months.

To cook Chorizo (sausage), thaw frozen sausage *just* to room temperature. Crumble sausage and brown thoroughly in a large heavy skillet over low to moderate heat, stirring occasionally so that sausage does not stick to the pan. Drain well. Use in scrambled eggs or mix with ground beef for tacos or Steak Relleno (see index) or as desired.

Cilantro Chicken
6 servings

Cilantro Chicken is an entree special that has been well received by our patrons. You can easily make it a specialty of yours if you prepare Salsa Ranchera in advance.

4 cups Salsa Ranchera (see index)
6 (7-ounce) boneless chicken breasts, skinned
1 cup flour
1 teaspoon white pepper or to taste
1 teaspoon cayenne pepper or to taste
1/2 cup *extra virgin* olive oil or butter or margarine
2 cups grated Monterey Jack or sharp Cheddar cheese
1 cup minced *fresh* or 1/2 cup dried cilantro
1/4 cup piñón (pinenuts) or peanuts for garnish
Black Beans'n Rice (see index)

Prepare Salsa Ranchera; set aside and keep warm (see note). In a zip-lock plastic or paper bag, combine flour, white pepper, and cayenne pepper. Add chicken, close bag tightly, and shake well to coat *each* chicken breast thoroughly; remove pieces, shaking excess flour from chicken. In a large heavy skillet, heat oil or melt butter or margarine over moderate heat. Add chicken and sauté quickly, turning constantly. Add Salsa Ranchera to pan; bring sauce to a brisk simmer. Arrange chicken pieces on individual plates, dividing evenly. Spoon Salsa Ranchera over *each* serving and then sprinkle cheese over sauce. Garnish *each* with piñón (pinenuts) and accompany with Black Beans n' Rice.

Note: Salsa Ranchera may be prepared 4 to 5 days in advance of recipe preparation, if desired.

Cordero Estante Asado
(Lista's Finest Rack of Lamb)
2 servings

Here at Lista's, we've been told we have the finest rack of lamb anywhere, possibly because many cooks hide the flavor of the meat with spices. I've tried — and I think accomplished — the complement in spices. When you read the list of spices, you may think I'm crazy — but try the recipe, you'll be delightfully surprised. Better yet, come to Lista's and allow us to send your taste buds to Heaven.

2 (12 to 16-ounce) racks of lamb, cleaned and Frenched (see note)
1/4 cup *extra virgin* olive oil
1 tablespoon lemon juice
1 tablespoon minced *fresh* or 1 1/2 teaspoons dried oregano
1 tablespoon minced *fresh* or 1 1/2 teaspoons dried mint leaves
1 tablespoon minced *fresh* or 1 1/2 teaspoons dried rosemary
1 tablespoon minced *fresh* or 1 1/2 teaspoons dried tarragon
1 tablespoon minced *fresh* or 1 1/2 teaspoons parsley
1 tablespoon paprika
1 tablespoon freshly ground black pepper or to taste
1 tablespoon salt or to taste
1 1/2 teaspoons cayenne pepper or to taste
Mint and/or Pepper Jelly for garnish

Prepare racks of lamb for roasting (see note). In a deep small bowl, combine oil, lemon juice, herbs, and spices, mixing well. With a pastry brush, liberally coat *each* rack of lamb, all sides, with the oil-herb mixture. Arrange lamb roast on a metal rack in a roaster or 13 x 9 x 2-inch baking dish; bake in the center of a preheated moderate oven (350°F.) for 14 minutes for medium rare and 20 minutes for medium doneness. With a sharp knife, carve roast into serving portions. Pass Mint and/or Pepper Jelly as accompaniments.

Note: Many butcher shops and meat departments of supermarkets will clean, trim, cut, and prepare racks of lamb for roasting.

Enchiladas
(Rolled or Stacked Filled Tortillas with Sauce)
4 to 6 servings

Here at Lista's we prepare our enchiladas two ways — stacked or rolled. Many different fillings may be used such as cooked shredded or ground beef, pulled chicken or turkey with sour cream, or the classic cheese and onion. Decisions, decisions! The best complements to my enchiladas of course are Frijóles Refritos and Spanish Rice.

4 cups Lista's Enchilada Sauce (see index)
About 1/2 cup cooking oil
2 cups prepared filling of choice
12 corn tortillas
1 cup shredded sharp Cheddar or Monterey Jack cheese
4 cups shredded lettuce
1 cup chopped peeled tomato
Thinly sliced or coarsely chopped pitted black olives for garnish
  (optional)
Frijóles Refritos (refried beans) (optional)
Spanish Rice (see index) (optional)

In a medium heavy saucepan, warm the sauce over low heat. In a large heavy skillet, heat oil to medium-low (325°F.); pan-fry tortillas, one at a time, *just* 5 seconds, making sure they remain very soft. Drain well on absorbent paper. Using a spatula or tongs, dip *each* warm tortilla into the warm sauce, coating *each* thoroughly. Spoon filling of choice over one side of *each* coated tortilla, dividing evenly. Roll tightly, jelly roll-style; arrange enchiladas in a 13 x 9 x 2-inch baking dish. Spoon any remaining sauce over enchiladas. Evenly sprinkle cheese over enchiladas. Or, dip enchiladas in the sauce and spread with filling as previously directed; stack tortillas, filling-side up, 2 to 3 tortillas to a stack, in a 9 x 9 x 2-inch or 11 x 7 x 2-inch baking dish. Spoon any remaining sauce over the enchiladas. Top *each* enchilada stack with cheese, dividing evenly. Bake in a preheated moderate oven (350°F.) for 8 to 10 minutes. To serve, arrange enchiladas, 2 to 3 rolled enchiladas or one stack to a serving, on heated dinner plates; sprinkle *each* serving with olives and accompany with Frijóles Refritos and Spanish Rice, if desired.

Enchiladas de Pollo con Salsa Blanca
(Chicken Enchiladas with New Mexican Jalapeño Cream Sauce)
4 to 6 servings

2 cups Pollo (chicken) (see page 60)
8 to 12 corn tortillas warmed in a preheated very slow oven (250ºF.)
1/2 cup butter or margarine
3/4 cup flour
1 teaspoon white pepper or to taste
Pinch of ground cumin

1 *fresh* jalapeño chile pepper, minced, or 1 1/2 teaspoons jalapeño chile
  pepper powder
2 cups milk
Salt to taste
Shredded Monterey Jack cheese as desired for garnish

Prepare chicken and tortillas in advance. In a medium heavy saucepan, melt butter over low heat. With a wire whisk, gradually blend in flour until mixture is a smooth paste. Add jalapeño chile pepper, white pepper, and cumin. Gradually add milk, blending well with the wire whisk. Cook, whisking constantly, over moderate heat until sauce is thickened and bubbly hot. Season with salt to taste.

To serve, spoon about 1/3 cup chicken onto *each* warm tortilla. Roll *each* filled tortilla tightly, jelly roll-style. Arrange rolled tortillas, two per serving, on *each* plate. Spoon about 1/3 cup hot jalapeño cream sauce over *each* serving. Garnish *each* with a liberal sprinkle of shredded Monterey Jack cheese. Serve immediately.

Variation: Arrange filled tortillas on heat-proof plates. Spoon sauce over each and garnish with shredded Monterey Jack cheese. Broil, 8 to 10 inches from heat source, for 2 to 3 minutes or until cheese melts. Serve immediately.

Masa Preparation

Masa Harina is a type of dried corn that has been very finely ground. It is the main ingredient used to make tamale dough or "Masa." If there is a tortilla factory nearby, you are probably familiar with fresh masa. Usually these factories will sell prepared masa by the pound. Remember that fresh masa is usually unflavored. It should be mixed with some kind of fat and/or meat stock to achieve a rich full flavor and proper consistency.

I prefer Masa Harina to fresh masa because of its easy availability and consistency in quality. The recipes that follow are all prepared with Masa Harina. Since the process of preparing the masa does not take much time, decide the filling to use and prepare it in advance.

The Art of Making Tamales

Having grown up in a predominantly Mexican neighborhood we called the West Side (Denver, Colorado), my first introduction to the tamale came at a very early age — probably five or six years. My mother has always said I loved hot spicy food at an unusually young age. That fact probably has had an influence with my chosen career.

As a young boy, I remember Mrs. Morales, located one block up on Ninth Street (from my boyhood home), would make dozens of edible steamed treasures filled with shredded pork and the most flavorful red chili. She will always be in my memory as the ultimate tamale expert. Since my childhood, I've tasted about every style of tamales, filled with a variety of meats, cheeses, and chiles. Of course, some were better than others, but all had their own distinctive flavor personalities.

As are most of the foods of New Mexico, tamales are fun to create. A little time consuming — yes — but, they're well worth the time and effort required to prepare them. Since they hold quite well, prepare a few dozen as people do in New Mexico in the traditional Mexican custom. Invite many willing and curious helpers to assist in making these little gift-wrapped works of art. Many hands will turn this time-consuming, sometimes tedious, job into a fun cooking lesson accompanied with plenty of laughs and conversation as well as enough tamales for every one involved to take home. Tamale making often becomes a family or friend reunion. For Mexicans, one can't find a better combination — food, family, and friends. Maybe sometimes too much!

Favorite Tamales
30 to 36 tamales
My favorite masa is the commercially prepared Maseca brand, Masa de Maiz or Corn Masa. Any type of corn masa is appropriate. Some have a coarse texture, while the Maseca brand is ground very fine similar to flour.

40 to 50 dried whole large corn husks
Warm water as needed
4 cups prepared masa
3 cups cooked beef or pork, or chicken pan drippings or cooking oil
3 tablespoons salt
2 tablespoons New Mexico-style (bright red) chili powder
1 tablespoon cayenne or ground hot red pepper
1/2 teaspoon ground cumin
4 cups Chicken or Shrimp Tamale Filling or other favorite filling
Favorite salsa as desired (optional)

Soften corn husks in a large container of warm water to cover for at least 1 hour. While husks are softening, prepare masa mixture. In an extra large bowl, combine 4 cups warm water, masa, meat drippings or oil, salt, chili powder, cayenne pepper, and cumin, mixing well with a wire whisk. Add additional water as necessary to achieve spreading consistency. (Sometimes masa is packed more tightly in a container than at other times.)

Drain all liquid from softened corn husks. Pat dry, a few at a time. Do not discard any torn or very small pieces as they may be used for patching tamales where necessary. Lay husks out flat with the narrow part of the husk pointed outward. Spoon about 4 ounces (1/2 cup) of masa onto *each* husk, spreading evenly from side to side into a 5 x 5-inch square, but not over the top of *each* husk. Leave about 2 inches of the husk tops uncoated. Spoon about 2 ounces (1/4 cup) of favorite filling lengthwise in a thin line over the masa. Loosely roll husks so that masa overlaps. Fold down the top uncoated flap of *each* husk and gently press to seal; turn *each* (over), placing flap underneath to keep *each* husk folded. Repeat process until all masa, filling, and husks are used. Tamales may be frozen to be cooked at a later time, if desired.

To cook, arrange in the top section of a double boiler equipped with steam vents. Place tamales loosely, staggering their placement to allow an even steam and air flow. Fill bottom half of double boiler halfway with hot water; bring water to a boil over high heat. Place tamale-filled top half over bottom of double boiler. Reduce heat slightly. Cover and steam-cook tamales for 40 to 50 minutes. Check water level in bottom of double boiler occasionally, adding hot water as necessary. Remove covered double boiler from heat; allow tamales to stand, covered, in steamer for at least 20 minutes.

To serve, gently unfold tamales and arrange 2 to 3 on *each* dinner plate. Spoon favorite salsa over *each* serving as desired.

Chicken Tamale Filling
about 5 cups

3 cups Pollo (see index)
2 cups Salsa Verde (see index)

Prepare Pollo and Salsa Verde in advance of tamale preparation; Pollo may be chilled for easier tamale assembling. In a medium bowl, combine Pollo and Salsa Verde, mixing well. Use as directed in tamale preparation.

Shrimp Tamale Filling
about 4 cups

3 cups deveined peeled raw shrimp, tails removed
1 cup Lista's Enchilada Sauce (see index)

Prepare shrimp, patting off any liquid with absorbent paper. In a medium bowl, combine shrimp and sauce, mixing well. Use as directed in tamale preparation.

Enchiladas Pescado
(Seafood Enchiladas)
4 servings

We put just about any type of seafood in these luscious enchiladas. My favorite filling for this tasty creation is the delicate combination of very small shrimp and backfin crabmeat. It's a recipe which has been designed for easy preparation.

8 ounces crabmeat
1 (1.8-ounce) package white sauce mix (see note)
2 1/4 cups milk
Jalapeño chile pepper powder to taste or 1 to 2 minced jalapeño
   chile peppers
White pepper to taste
About 3 quarts boiling salted water
8 ounces *very small* shrimp or bay scallops
12 soft corn tortillas
1 cup shredded Monterey Jack cheese
Calabacitas (see index)
Thin lemon wedges and peeled avocado slices immediately sprinkled
   with lemon juice

Pick over crabmeat, removing any shell or cartilage; set aside. In a medium heavy saucepan, prepare white sauce mix combined with milk according to package directions. Add jalapeño chile pepper powder or chile peppers and white pepper, mixing well. In a large heavy saucepan, cook shrimp or scallops in boiling salted water for 3 minutes or until shrimp or scallops turn opaque in color; drain well. *Do not overcook, as seafood will become tough.*

Pan-fry tortillas (see Enchiladas, page 50); drain well. *Tortillas should remain soft and not become crisp.* Place 4 tortillas on a baking sheet; spoon about 1 to 2 tablespoons shrimp or scallops and 1 to 2 tablespoons crabmeat onto each tortilla. Sprinkle each with 2 tablespoons cheese. Repeat process twice more for *each* tortilla, stacking filled tortillas, one atop the other, 2 tortillas to a stack. Spoon prepared sauce over *each* set of stacked tortillas. Sprinkle additional grated cheese over the sauce. Bake, uncovered, in a preheated moderate oven (350°F.) for 4 to 6 minutes. Cut *each* into 4 wedges and serve immediately. Accompany with Calabacitas, if desired and garnish *each* serving with thin lemon wedges and avocado slices.

Note: Preferably use Knorr brand white sauce mix. Or, prepare 2 cups favorite white (Bechamel) sauce recipe.

Holiday Turkey with Dad's Stuffing
8 to 10 servings

There is nothing Mexican or Southwest about this recipe — you can't live only on spicy food.

1 (12 to 16-pound) turkey
8 ounces medium or hot-spiced bulk pork sausage or Chorizo (sausage) (see index)
8 ounces sliced bacon
1 bunch celery, chopped, including leaves
1 cup minced peeled onion
2 (16-ounce) packages herbed stuffing mix
4 cups chicken broth
1 tablespoon white pepper or to taste

Remove giblets and neck from body cavity. Rinse turkey and pat dry with absorbent paper. Cover and set aside while preparing stuffing.

In a medium heavy skillet, pan-fry sausage over low to moderate heat, crumbling into small pieces, until lightly browned; drain well, retaining drippings from sausage in skillet. Set aside sausage. Pan-fry bacon in hot sausage drippings over moderate heat until crisp; drain well on absorbent paper. Crumble bacon and set aside. Transfer hot pan drippings to a large heavy skillet; add celery and onion. Sauté vegetables over moderate heat until *just* tender but not browned. In a large bowl, combine crumbled sausage, bacon, celery, onion, stuffing mix, chicken broth, and pepper, mixing well. Mixture will be of a sticky consistency.

Fill neck cavity loosely with stuffing. *Do not pack, as stuffing expands during roasting.* Fold neck skin over dressing in cavity opening and securing to back with skewers. Loosely stuff body cavity. Lock wings behind the back (akimbo) and tie drumsticks to tail with heavy string. Insert meat thermometer into the thickest part of thigh muscle. Place turkey on a metal rack in a large roaster. Cover loosely with aluminum foil (shiny side in), leaving openings at either end. Allow a hole in the foil for the meat thermometer. Roast in a preheated slow oven (325°F.) until done, about 4 1/2 to 5 hours (allow 20 to 25 minutes per pound for roasting); meat thermometer will register 180° to 185°F. Remove foil about 45 minutes before the end of the roasting period to ensure even browning of bird. Baste turkey liberally with pan juices.

Cut strings holding legs when two-thirds done. Remove turkey from oven when done and cover tightly with aluminum foil. Drain pan juices and for gravy; skim off excess fat. Allow to rest at room temperature for 20 to 25 minutes for easier carving. Prepare gravy, if desired. Arrange turkey on a heated platter, garnish as desired, and serve. Pass gravy in sauceboat, if desired.

Huevos con Chorizo
(Eggs with Spicy Sausage)
6 servings

In order to serve this dish for breakfast, you will have to prepare the chorizo in advance. It's a wonderful breakfast or brunch entree which is also easy to prepare.

8 ounces Chorizo (sausage) (see index)
3 tablespoons *extra virgin* olive oil or butter or margarine
1 small onion, peeled and cut into 1 1/2 to 2-inch strips
1 small green bell pepper, cored, seeded, and cut into thin strips
1/2 firm *ripe* medium tomato, chopped
8 eggs, lightly beaten
Chili Verde (see index) (optional)
Charro Beans (see index)
Soft flour or corn tortillas, as desired, warmed in a very slow
    oven (275°F.)

Prepare homemade Chorizo (sausage) according to directions or use commercial Chorizo. In a large heavy skillet, heat oil or melt butter or margarine over moderate heat; add sausage, crumble, and cook, stirring frequently, until sausage is lightly browned. Add onion and bell pepper; continue to sauté for about 30 seconds, until vegetables are *just* tender but crisp. Add eggs; continue to cook, stirring constantly, until desired doneness, about 2 to 3 minutes. Eggs may be garnished with hot Chili Verde, if desired. Serve immediately with warm tortillas and Charro Beans.

Huachinango a la Ruben
(Red Snapper with Garlic Butter)
4 servings

4 whole red snapper, *each* about 1 3/4 pounds, cleaned (see note)
7 garlic cloves, peeled and divided
1 medium onion, peeled and very thinly sliced
6 tablespoons *fresh* lime juice, divided
1/4 cup minced *fresh* or 2 tablespoons dried cilantro, divided
1 1/2 teaspoons minced *fresh* or 3/4 teaspoon dried oregano, divided
Salt and freshly ground black pepper to taste
4 medium baking potatoes
3/4 cup clarified butter (see note)
1/2 cup *extra virgin* olive oil, divided
About 1 cup flour
Sprigs of cilantro and lime wedges for garnish

Prepare fish for cooking. Heads and tails may be left intact, if desired. With a French knife, mince 4 garlic cloves; set aside. Purée remaining 3 garlic cloves, covered, in a blender container at high speed. Arrange fish in a 12 x 8 x 2-inch baking dish; evenly spread *each*, both sides, with puréed garlic. Sprinkle *each* with about 1 1/2 tablespoons lime juice, 1 1/2 to 2 teaspoons cilantro, 1/2 teaspoon oregano, and salt and pepper to taste. Cover and refrigerate for 3 hours to allow fish to absorb the marinade flavors.

About 1 hour before serving, brush potatoes lightly with oil; bake in a preheated moderate oven (375°F.) until potatoes are fork tender, about 50 to 60 minutes.

Drain fish thoroughly. Strain marinade; reserve onions and marinade separately and set aside. In a small heavy skillet, heat butter to foaming. Add remaining oil, marinated onion slices, and minced garlic; sauté onion and garlic over moderate heat until tender but not browned. Season with salt and pepper to taste. Strain, dividing butter in half, reserving one half and keeping warm until serving time. Reserve onion slices and keep warm.

On a sheet of wax paper, dredge fish in flour, coating *each* well; return fish to baking dish. Evenly drizzle the unreserved portion of strained butter over the fish. Bake, uncovered, in a preheated moderate oven (375°F.) for 10 minutes, or until fish are opaque in color and *just* flake easily with a fork. Turn oven setting to broil and broil fish, 8 to 10 inches from heat source, turning (over) fish once, for 2 to 3 minutes or until fish are lightly browned. Remove fish and potatoes from oven. Cut an X into the top of *each* potato with a sharp knife; gently squeeze potatoes to open *each*. Arrange a snapper and a baked potato on *each* dinner plate. Drizzle warm reserved butter over *each* fish and in *each* potato. Garnish *each* with sautéed onion slices, a sprig of cilantro, and lime wedges.

Note: 8 to 10 ounces of red snapper filet may be used for each serving in place of a whole red snapper. Swordfish or shrimp may be substituted for red snapper, if desired.

Note: To clarify butter, melt butter in a small heavy saucepan over low heat. Pour melted butter into a small bowl and allow to cool to room temperature. Skim off the pure fat collecting at the top of the bowl and discard the remaining solids and water.

Pechuga
(Grilled Chicken Sandwich)
1 serving

**5 ounces grilled boneless chicken breast, skin removed (see page 46
 for grilling instructions)**
1 large Kaiser roll, split in half and toasted
1/2 cup shredded Monterey Jack cheese
Crisp leaf lettuce
1 slice firm *ripe* tomato
2 to 3 pickle slices
2 to 3 slices peeled *ripe* avocado sprinkled with lemon juice

Prepare chicken breast. Arrange chicken on the bottom half of a Kaiser roll on an oven-proof plate. Top with cheese. Broil, 6 to 8 inches from heat source, or bake in a preheated moderate oven (375°F.) until cheese is melted, about 3 minutes for broiling and 5 to 6 minutes for baking. Arrange top half of roll, cut-side up, next to chicken; garnish top half of roll with leaf lettuce, tomato slice, pickle slices, and avocado slices. Serve immediately.

Huevos Rancheros con Chili Verde
(Ranch-style Eggs with Green Chili)
1 serving

Huevos Rancheros is probably the most popular breakfast entree in Mexico. What a zesty way to begin a morning!!! There are as many variations as there are cooks — included here is Lista's favorite recipe for the traditional egg dish.

1 corn tortilla
About 1/4 cup hot cooking oil for frying tortilla
2 eggs
About 1 to 2 tablespoons hot cooking oil or butter or margarine, melted
1/2 cup Chili Verde, heated (see index)
1/2 to 1 cup Frijóles Refritos (refried beans), heated (see index)
1/2 to 1 cup Spanish Rice, heated (see index)
1/4 cup shredded Monterey Jack, or sharp Cheddar, or Swiss cheese
Additional flour or corn tortillas warmed in a preheated very
    slow oven (250°F.) for garnish

In a medium heavy skillet, pan-fry the tortilla in hot oil, until cooked but still soft, about 30 seconds per side; drain well on absorbent paper. In a small heavy skillet, pan-fry eggs in 1 to 2 tablespoons hot oil over low to moderate heat to desired degree of doneness and style ("sunny-side-up, basted, "over-easy", etc.). Arrange fried corn tortilla on an individual plate and top with cooked eggs. Spoon heated Chili Verde over eggs. Spoon Frijóles Refritos and then the Spanish Rice adjacent to the eggs; sprinkle the cheese over the beans. Garnish with additional warmed flour or corn tortillas. Serve immediately.

Huevos Rancheros con Salsa Roja
(Ranch-style Eggs with Hot Red Sauce)
1 serving

This recipe is a completely different style from the traditional Huevos Rancheros. I find Home Fries (potatoes) (Papas de la Casa) go well with this dish.

1 corn tortilla
About 1/4 cup hot cooking oil for frying tortilla
2 eggs
1/2 cup Lista's Hot Sauce (see index)
1/3 cup shredded Monterey Jack cheese
1/4 cup cooked black beans or Frijóles Refritos (refried beans),
    heated (see index)
2 to 3 slices peeled avocado slices sprinkled with lemon or lime juice
    for garnish
Additional 2 to 3 corn tortillas for garnish, warmed in a preheated very
    slow oven (250°F.)

In a medium heavy skillet, pan-fry 1 corn tortilla in hot oil until crisp, about 30 to 45 seconds per side; drain well on absorbent paper. Pan-fry eggs as directed in Huevos Rancheros con Chili Verde. Arrange crisp tortilla on an individual plate; top with cooked eggs. Spoon sauce over the eggs and sprinkle with cheese. Serve with black beans and garnish with avocado slices and 2 to 3 additional heated soft corn tortillas.

Lista's Fajitas
8 servings

4 pounds beef skirt steak, gristle and fat removed (see note)
4 garlic cloves, peeled and minced
1 jalapeño chile pepper, cut into strips
2 cups water
1 cup *extra virgin* olive oil
1/4 cup tequila
1/4 cup *fresh* lime or lemon juice
1/2 cup minced *fresh* cilantro or parsley
2 tablespoons liquid smoke
2 tablespoons freshly ground black pepper or to taste
2 tablespoons salt or to taste
2 teaspoons minced *fresh* or 1 teaspoon dried oregano
3 medium onions, peeled and cut into thin vertical wedges
3 medium green bell peppers, cored, seeded, and cut into small pieces
2 firm *ripe* tomatoes, cored and cut into thick wedges
2 cups Pico de Gallo (see index)
2 cups Lista's Guacamole (see index)
Corn or flour tortillas, as desired, warmed in a preheated very
    slow oven (250°F.)

With a sharp knife, cut steak into eight (6-ounce) pieces. Pound *each* flat with a meat mallet; set aside. In a blender container, combine the next 11 ingredients; cover and blend at high speed until mixture is smooth. Pour marinade into a large rectangular pan or glass casserole. Add beef, coating *each* piece well with the marinade; cover and refrigerate for 2 to 12 hours.

Remove meat from marinade, draining well. Arrange beef on a grill rack, 8 to 10 inches above medium coals (ash gray and glowing); grill about 3 minutes per side for medium rare or until desired degree of doneness is achieved. Arrange vegetables in a vegetable grill basket or on a sheet of heavy-duty aluminum foil placed atop the grill rack. Grill vegetables about 1 minute, turning once; allow vegetables to remain firm. *Do not overcook.* Meat and vegetables may be sautéed in 2 tablespoons hot olive oil in a sauté pan or heavy skillet to desired degree of doneness, if desired.

To serve, cut *each* piece of grilled steak into thin strips. Arrange steak strips and vegetables on individual plates, dividing evenly. Serve with Lista's Guacamole, Pico de Gallo, and tortillas, allowing guests to roll their own fajitas.

Note: May use beef sirloin, or top round, or tenderloin steak, if desired.

Lista's Langusta
(Lista's Lobster Tail)
4 servings

Occasionally lobster tail appears on Lista's menu — yes, lobster, and in more than one way of preparation — broiled in the shell, or grilled out of the shell for our Surf n' Turf Fajitas. Or, how about a wonderful seafood salad which includes lobster? Below is one example of preparing the tasty crustacean. We serve our lobster tails with Black Beans n' Rice or Red Pepper and Garlic Butter Sauce.

4 (7 to 8-ounce) *fresh* or frozen rock lobster tails (see note)
Butter or margarine as desired, melted
Paprika as desired
Cayenne pepper as desired
Seafood seasoning as desired (see note)
4 cups Salsa Ranchera or Chilpotle Pepper Sauce (optional) (see index)
1 cup shredded Monterey Jack cheese (optional) (see note)
Red Pepper and Garlic Butter Sauce

With a sharp knife, cut *each* lobster tail lengthwise through the underside shell three-fourths into the lobster meat; spread *each* shell open and carefully pull out meat, leaving the tip of the lobster tail intact in the shell. Close shell tightly and drape lobster meat *(in one piece)* back over *each* shell to give an appearance of *each* tail bursting out of its shell *(this technique does take practice)*.

Arrange lobster tails on a rack in a shallow baking or broiler pan. Brush *each* tail with butter and sprinkle *each* with paprika, cayenne pepper, black pepper, and seafood seasoning to taste. Bake in a preheated moderate oven (350°F.) for 10 to 12 minutes. *Do not overbake as lobster will become tough.* While lobster tails are baking, heat prepared Salsa Ranchera or Chilpotle Pepper Sauce in a medium heavy saucepan to a simmer, or prepare Red Pepper and Garlic Butter Sauce to serve as an accompaniment.

Note: If using frozen lobster tails, thaw completely before using.

Note: Preferably use Old Bay Seafood Seasoning.

Red Pepper and Garlic Butter Sauce
about 1 cup

1 cup butter or margarine (see note)
2 to 3 garlic cloves, peeled
2 chile pequin or pasilla chile peppers
1 tablespoon *fresh* lemon juice

In a small heavy saucepan, melt butter over low heat. Add garlic, chiles, and lemon juice; *heat through but do not boil.* Remove garlic and chiles; discard. Divide sauce into individual butter warmers with warming candles; serve as an accompaniment to lobster and other seafood. Keep sauce warm over lighted warming candles or other warming device.

Note: Margarine may be used; however, the flavor will not be the same.

Lista's Southwestern Skillet
1 serving

For a brunch with a southwestern flair, try Lista's popular week-end late breakfast or lunch entree.

1 corn tortilla
1/2 to 1 cup Papas de la Casa (see index)
2 eggs
1/2 cup Chili Verde (see index)
1/4 cup shredded sharp Cheddar cheese
2 slices crisp-cooked bacon
Fresh fruit of choice for garnish

Pan-fry tortilla and prepare eggs as directed in Huevos Rancheros con Chili Verde (see index). Place tortilla on an oval cast-iron skillet or other oven-proof individual serving plate. Arrange potatoes over the tortilla; top with prepared eggs. Spoon Chili Verde over the eggs and sprinkle with cheese. Bake in a preheated hot oven (400°F.) for 1 minute, *just* until cheese is melted. Arrange bacon aside the tortilla and garnish with *fresh* fruit of choice.

Marisqueta con Chorizo
(Boiled Rice with Sausage)
4 to 6 servings

2 tablespoons cooking oil or lard
8 ounces Chorizo (sausage) (see index)
1/4 cup chopped peeled onion
4 cups cooked long-grain white rice
2 cups chopped peeled firm *ripe* tomatoes
1 tablespoon minced *fresh* or 1 1/2 teaspoons dried cilantro

In a large heavy skillet, heat oil or melt lard. Crumble Chorizo (sausage) into skillet over low heat. Add onion; cook, stirring constantly, until *just* tender. Add rice and tomatoes, mixing well; heat through. Add cilantro, tossing mixture lightly to mix. Serve immediately.

Machaca
(Leftovers)
4 servings

Due to leftovers remaining from the previous evening's meal, you'll find this dish or something very similar to it in most cultures. The Italians call the mixture a fritata, mixing meatballs or sausage with onions and green peppers and holding the combination together with scrambled egg. Egg Fu Yung is the same dish with a Chinese flavor, substituting cooked shredded pork or shrimp. The Mexicans call their specialty Machaca — a wonderful entrée to serve for breakfast or brunch guests.

6 eggs
2 Anaheim mild green chile peppers, roasted and peeled (see page 73, 81), and cut into thin long strips
1 medium green bell pepper, cored, seeded, and cut into long thin strips
1 medium firm *ripe* tomato, chopped
1 small onion, peeled and cut into thin long strips or coarsely chopped
1/4 cup hot cooking oil or butter or margarine, melted
8 ounces (about 1 cup) shredded or cut-up cooked beef roast or air-dried beef
1 teaspoon freshly ground black pepper or to taste
Salt to taste
Flour or corn tortillas as desired, warmed in a preheated very slow oven (250°F.)
Frijóles Refritos (refried beans) (see index)

In a large bowl, beat eggs lightly; set aside. In a large heavy skillet, sauté roasted chile peppers, bell pepper, tomato, and onion in oil or butter over moderate heat until *just* tender. Add meat, mixing well; season with pepper and salt to taste. Reduce heat. Pour beaten eggs over mixture, scrambling egg mixture in a circular motion with a fork or wooden spoon over low heat until *just* "set" and firm. *Do not overcook.* Spoon onto heated plates, dividing evenly, and serve with warm soft tortillas and Frijóles Refritos.

Meat Filling for Tacos, Enchiladas, or Burritos
(enough meat filling for 16 to 20 tacos, 16 to 20 enchiladas, or 12 burritos)

This simple meat filling lends itself well as a filling for tacos, enchiladas, or burritos.

2 pounds lean ground beef
2 tablespoons New Mexico-style (bright red) chili powder
1 tablespoon salt or to taste
1 teaspoon ground cumin
1 teaspoon minced peeled garlic or garlic powder
1 (6-ounce) can tomato juice

In a medium heavy skillet, brown ground beef thoroughly over moderate heat, stirring frequently; drain off any meat drippings. Add seasonings, mixing well. Mash with a potato masher, if desired, to break-up any large pieces of ground beef. Add tomato juice, mixing well. Use as a filling for tacos, enchiladas, or burritos.

Blue Corn Enchiladas New Mexican-Style
4 servings

New Mexican-style enchiladas are usually stacked, not rolled. The fillings are layered between soft corn tortillas and then smothered with a rich medium-spiced enchilada sauce popular in northern New Mexico. Here we use blue corn tortillas, which have become trendy in the last few years.

4 cups Salsa Verde (see index), divided
1/2 recipe Pollo (chicken) (see index), divided
16 blue corn tortillas, divided (see note)
About 2 cups hot cooking oil
1/2 cup chopped peeled onion, divided
2 cups shredded Monterey Jack cheese
4 cups shredded iceberg lettuce, divided
Chopped firm *ripe* tomatoes for garnish
Sour cream for garnish
Charro Beans (see index)

Prepare Salsa Verde; set aside. Prepare chicken filling; set aside. In a large heavy skillet, pan-fry tortillas in oil over moderate heat, about 30 seconds per side; drain well on absorbent paper. *Tortillas should not become crisp, but remain soft.* In a medium heavy skillet, heat Salsa Verde to *just* simmering over low heat. Using a spatula or tongs, dip 4 tortillas, one at a time, into the sauce, coating *each* well. Arrange tortillas on a baking sheet. Sprinkle *each* with chicken filling, onions, and cheese, and shredded lettuce. Repeat dipping and layering process three times more. Spoon additional sauce over the top tortillas and use only chicken and then cheese for the top enchilada layer. The finished enchiladas may be served warm, or transfer to a preheated moderate oven (350°F.) and bake for 4 to 5 minutes or until cheese is melted. Serve immediately garnished with additional shredded lettuce, chopped tomato, and sour cream. Serve Charro Beans on the side.

Note: Blue corn tortillas available at most specialty food stores.

Molé Poblano
(Chicken Stew in Hot Sauce with Chocolate)
6 servings

Molé Poblano is one of the oldest recipes existing in the Mexican cuisine. The word Molé comes from the Nahuatl root mulli, which means sauce. The sauce is believed to have been invented in a pueblo convent. Today we usually prepare this dish for special occasions such as weddings and baptisms. The list of ingredients is long but should not be discouraging — a blender, a stockpot, and a heavy skillet are the only utensils required to cook this wonderful entree.

2 (2 1/2 to 3-pound) broiler/frying chickens, cut into serving pieces
Water as needed, divided
10 black peppercorns, divided
2 bay leaves
1/2 medium onion, peeled and coarsely chopped
Salt to taste
4 dried pasilla chile peppers
4 dried mulato chile peppers
3 dried ancho chile peppers
4 tablespoons hot cooking oil, divided
4 garlic cloves, peeled
2 firm *ripe* small tomatoes
2 corn tortillas, cut in pieces
1/2 cup lightly salted peanuts
2 tablespoons toasted sesame seeds
2 tablespoons dark seedless raisins
1/4 teaspoon cinnamon
2 ounces (6 tablespoons) Mexican-style spiced chocolate (see note)
   or 2 ounces (2 squares) semi-sweet chocolate
1 tablespoon sugar
Salt to taste
Cantina Nuts (see index) for garnish

Place chicken in a Dutch oven or medium heavy stockpot; add water to cover, 6 peppercorns, bay leaves, onion, and salt. Bring to a boil over moderate heat; reduce temperature and simmer, partially covered, for 1 hour.

While chicken is cooking, prepare sauce. Rinse chile peppers; dry thoroughly on absorbent paper. In a large heavy saucepan, heat 3 tablespoons oil; add chiles and pan-fry about 5 minutes, turning constantly. Drain well. In a blender container, combine chiles and 1 cup water; cover and blend at high speed until peppers are puréed. Press mixture through a sieve to eliminate peel; set aside. Combine garlic, tomatoes, and onion in a blender container; cover and blend until smooth. Transfer mixture to a small bowl and set aside.

In a small heavy skillet, heat remaining 1 tablespoon oil; add tortilla pieces, peanuts, sesame seeds, and raisins; sauté over moderate heat, stirring frequently, until mixture is lightly toasted. Drain well. Transfer mixture to a blender container. Add cinnamon, cover, and blend at medium speed, adding chicken broth from the chicken pot as necessary. Add sugar and chocolate, cover, and continue to blend until mixture is smooth.

Combine all purées together in a large Dutch oven or medium heavy stock-pot. Simmer, uncovered, over low heat for 1 1/2 hours, adding chicken broth as needed to keep sauce from becoming too thick. Drain hot chicken; reserve remaining broth for other use.

To serve, arrange chicken pieces in a clay pot on a platter; spoon sauce over chicken. Or, arrange chicken pieces on individual plates and spoon sauce over individual servings. Garnish *each* with Cantina Nuts.

Note: Available in Mexican food specialty stores as a wrapped, scored, unsweetened chocolate, spiced with a touch of cinnamon flavor.

Pez Espada
(Swordfish Santa Fe-style)
4 servings

In my opinion, this cajun-inspired recipe is the best way to prepare meaty fish. You must remember this dish may smoke-up your kitchen, depending upon the efficiency of the house exhaust system. Please don't let this inconvenience deter you from preparation as the flavor of the fish is well worth some choking and coughing — just kidding! You will need a large flat cast-iron plate placed over a full flame — just as hot as you can get it!

1 tablespoon paprika
1 tablespoon New Mexico-style (bright red) chili powder
1 tablespoon cayenne pepper
1 tablespoon freshly ground black pepper
1 tablespoon granulated dried garlic or 3 to 4 garlic cloves,
    peeled and minced
2 teaspoons minced *fresh* or 1 teaspoon dried oregano
1 teaspoon salt or to taste
1 teaspoon ground cumin
1/2 cup *extra virgin* olive oil or butter or margarine, melted
4 (8 to 10-ounce) *fresh* or thawed frozen swordfish steaks
Charro Beans (see index) (optional)
Posole (see index) (optional)

Combine the first 8 ingredients together in a small bowl, mixing well. With a pastry brush, liberally brush *each* swordfish steak, both sides, with olive oil, butter, or margarine. Spread herb-spice mixture over a sheet of wax paper; dredge fish steaks in mixture, coating *each* well. Set aside. Preheat a cast-iron plate or large heavy skillet over high heat. Add fish steaks, two at a time, to hot plate or skillet; sear (blacken) for 2 minutes. Turn (over) steaks and sear for an additional 2 minutes, blackening swordfish. Repeat process for 2 remaining fish steaks. *(Be careful when turning fish steaks, as any spice falling from fish reacts similar to cinders for a fire.)* Serve immediately, accompanied with Charro Beans and Posole, if desired.

Pollo
(Chicken)
*(enough filling for 16 tacos, tostadas, or chile rellenos,
or 8 to 10 burritos, chimichangas, or taco salads)*

Chicken served in many ways is the most popular entree at Lista's. I use only skin-less boneless breast meat in my cooking.

2 New Mexico green chile peppers, thinly sliced
1 medium onion, peeled and chopped
1 chicken bouillon cube
8 cups water
1 tablespoon paprika
1 tablespoon minced *fresh* or 1 1/2 teaspoons dried cilantro
1 1/2 teaspoons white pepper or to taste
1 1/2 teaspoons granulated dried garlic or 2 to 3 garlic cloves,
    peeled and minced
1 1/2 teaspoons celery salt
1 1/2 teaspoons chili powder
5 pounds boneless chicken breasts, skin removed and cut into thin strips

In a Dutch oven or medium heavy stockpot, combine the first 10 in-gredients; bring to a rolling boil over moderate heat. Add chicken, reduce heat, and simmer until *just* done, about 5 to 7 minutes. Strain liquid, reserv-ing for another use. Serve as desired.

Pollo sin Nombre
(Chicken with No Name)
4 servings

During a recent trip to Mexico, Kathy and I discovered a beautiful restaurant with no name — cleverly so named, Restaurant Sin Nombre (No Name). I tried a wonderful tasting chicken dish. Giving credit where credit is due, I have reconstructed what I tasted.

1/2 cup flour
2 teaspoons salt or to taste
1 teaspoon white pepper or to taste
1 teaspoon cayenne or ground dried hot red pepper
4 (7 to 8-ounce) boneless whole chicken breasts, skin removed
1/4 cup hot *extra virgin* olive oil or butter or margarine, melted, divided
1 large green bell pepper, cored, seeded, and cut into thin strips
1/2 cup dry white wine
2 cups heavy cream
Hot cooked rice or pasta of choice

Combine the first 4 ingredients together on a sheet of wax paper or in a brown or a plastic zip-lock bag; dredge chicken pieces in the mixture, coat-ing *each* lightly. In a large heavy skillet, brown chicken lightly in 2 tablespoons olive oil over low to moderate heat, turning chicken frequently. In a separate large heavy skillet, sauté green pepper in 2 tablespoons olive oil over moderate heat for 1 minute. Add chicken and wine. Reduce heat and gradually blend in cream; continue to simmer, uncovered, for about 5 minutes, reducing the sauce. Ad*just* seasonings to taste. Serve immediately over hot cooked rice or pasta of choice.

Pollo y Langusta
(Chicken and Lobster)
4 *servings*

I wish I could take credit for this wonderful rich-tasting entree; however, I discovered it in one of our favorite restaurants, Tio Pepe's, located in Baltimore. This is my interpretation of that marvelous recipe.

1 1/4 pounds boneless chicken breasts, skin removed and cut
  into 1/2-inch thick strips
1 pound plus 2 ounces *raw* lobster tail meat, removed from shell and
  cut into 3/4 to 1-inch pieces (may also use claw meat, if desired)
  (see note)
3 garlic cloves, peeled
1 large sweet red bell pepper, cored, seeded, and cut into thin strips
6 tablespoons *extra virgin* olive oil
6 tablespoons dry red wine
2 cups heavy cream
Salt and freshly ground black pepper to taste
Hot cooked rice or pasta of choice
Minced *fresh* cilantro for garnish
Chilpotle Pepper Squash or Gail's Favorite Fried Cabbage (see index)

Prepare chicken, lobster, garlic, and sweet red pepper for cooking. Heat oil in a large heavy skillet or wok to medium (350°F.). Add chicken, lobster, garlic, and sweet red pepper; sauté for *just* 2 to 3 minutes, stirring constantly. Add cream and wine, blending well; bring to a boil, stirring constantly. Reduce heat and allow liquid to reduce by one-third. Season with salt and pepper to taste. Serve over hot cooked rice or pasta of choice. Garnish *each* serving with a sprinkle of minced cilantro. Accompany with Chilpotle Pepper Squash or Gail's Favorite Fried Cabbage.

Note: 4 (6-ounce) lobster tails will yield about 16 to 18 ounces raw lobster meat.

Pork Adobo
(Spiced Pork Shoulder With Rice)
4 to 6 servings

Just the thought of this wonderful dish brings back so many memories of my father in our small kitchen of my boyhood home in Denver where he would go so often to do the cooking magic only he could perform. Effortlessly he would wave a chef's knife over a pot as a magician over a hat and presto there was an unforgettable aroma and flavor.

2 pounds *fresh* pork shoulder (butt), cut into 1-inch cubes
1/4 cup hot cooking oil
2 garlic cloves, peeled and minced
2 cups hot water
1/2 cup cider vinegar
3 tablespoons paprika
1 tablespoon pickling spice
1 tablespoon whole black peppercorns
1 teaspoon grated peeled ginger root
Salt to taste
Hot cooked rice as desired

In a heavy 3-quart saucepan, brown pork in oil over moderate heat, turning constantly, about 5 minutes. Add garlic and continue to sauté an additional minute. Add water, cover, and cook for 10 minutes. Add remaining ingredients, except rice, and continue to cook, partially covered, for 10 to 15 minutes. *Just* before serving, remove peppercorns. Serve over hot cooked rice.

Pulled or Shredded Beef
(enough filling for 16 to 20 tacos, 16 to 20 enchiladas, or 12 burritos)

2 pounds beef flank or top round steak, cut into thin 2-inch strips
1 medium onion, peeled and cut into thin strips
3 cups hot water
2 cups chopped firm *ripe* tomatoes
3 tablespoons New Mexico-style (bright red) chili powder
3 tablespoons salt or to taste
2 tablespoons granulated dried garlic or 4 garlic cloves, peeled
    and minced
2 teaspoons minced *fresh* or 1 teaspoon dried Mexican oregano (see note)

In a large heavy saucepan, combine beef, onion, and water. Bring to a boil, covered, over high heat; reduce temperature and simmer, covered, for 2 hours. Drain well; add remaining ingredients to meat in saucepan, mixing well. Return to low heat, covered, for an additional 10 minutes. Spread mixture in one layer over a baking sheet; shred meat with the tines of 2 forks. Use as a filling for Taquitos or try with eggs in Machaca.

Note: More pungent in flavor and lighter in color. Available in most grocery stores.

Rosa Camarón
(Grilled Shrimp in Spicy Red Sauce)
4 servings

The original version of this recipe was first developed at the El Torrito restaurant in California over twenty five years ago. Although I have added some variations, the presentation is still as colorful as that of the original.

4 cups Spanish Rice (see index)
16 to 20 jumbo (16-20 *count*) shrimp, peeled and deveined, tails intact
8 to 10 bacon slices, *each* cut in half
4 (10 to 12-inch) bamboo skewers
1/2 cup Salsa Aduvada (see index) or hot-spiced barbecue sauce of choice
4 peeled *fresh* or canned pineapple slices, cut into rings (see note)
Leaf lettuce, cored, cleaned, dried, and separated into individual
    leaves, as desired, for garnish
4 Maraschino cherries for garnish
Cilantro Cocktail Sauce

Prepare Spanish Rice; keep warm, covered, while preparing shrimp. Or, reheat *just* before serving. Prepare shrimp and bacon for grilling. Wrap a bacon half-slice around *each* shrimp. Thread 4 to 5 wrapped shrimp through the middle of *each* shrimp onto *each* skewer. Arrange skewers on a grill rack, 8 to 10 inches above medium charcoal (ash gray and glowing) in a grill fire box. Grill, basting shrimp constantly with Aduvada Sauce and turning skewers occasionally, about 2 to 3 minutes per side. *Allow shrimp to char slightly, being careful they do not burn.* While shrimp are grilling, also grill pineapple slices, about 1 minute per side.

Line *each* of 4 individual medium bowls with leaf lettuce; spoon hot Spanish Rice into the bowls, dividing evenly. Arrange a grilled pineapple slice over *each* serving of rice; garnish with a Maraschino cherry in the center of *each* pineapple ring. Remove grilled shrimp from skewers, arranging 4 to 5 around *each* pineapple ring over the rice, tails pointing inward toward pineapple. Serve immediately. Pass Cilantro Cocktail Sauce in a sauceboat.

Note: Choose a firm ripe pineapple with a good pineapple aroma and more golden than green in color. If canned pineapple is used, choose pineapple in its-own-juice rather than sweetened pineapple, as it tastes closer to fresh pineapple.

Cilantro Cocktail Sauce
about 2 cups

1 3/4 cups ketchup
3 tablespoons lemon juice
2 tablespoons minced *fresh* or 1 tablespoon dried cilantro
4 teaspoons freshly grated horseradish
1/2 teaspoon Tabasco sauce or to taste

In a small bowl, combine all ingredients, blending well. Cover and chill thoroughly in the refrigerator. Serve sauce *very* cold.

Tortilla Español
(Spanish Omelette)
one large or 2 medium servings

3 eggs
Few drops water
1 tablespoon butter or margarine
1/3 cup plus 1 tablespoon shredded Monterey Jack cheese, divided
1/2 to 3/4 cup Frijóles Refritos (refried beans) (see index)
Salsa Ranchera (see index)

In a small bowl, combine eggs and water; beat lightly with a fork. Melt butter in a small heavy skillet or 7-inch omelette pan over low heat. Add egg mixture to skillet. Cook egg mixture until *just* set, stirring gently in a circular motion with a fork for a few seconds. Evenly sprinkle 1/3 cup cheese over the omelette. With a rubber spatula, carefully lift one side of the omelet from the pan, folding over and over until the omelette is 3 inches wide. Transfer omelette to an oven-proof plate. Bake in a preheated slow oven (300°F.) for 4 to 6 minutes. *Do not overbake.* Place Frijóles Refritos to the side of the omelette and top with 1 tablespoon cheese. Serve immediately. Pass Salsa Ranchera in a sauceboat to spoon over omelette.

Ribs of Fire
4 servings

People come from many places to challenge my Ribs of Fire. At Lista's we prepare a full rack of baby back (pork) ribs with an unforgettable sauce. I hope to bottle the sauce some day. This recipe is not that of the ribs we serve at the restaurant, but a taste-tempter for readers to visit us in Virginia Beach.

5 pounds (4 racks, *each* abut 1 1/4 pounds) baby back (pork) ribs (see note)
4 cups water
2 cups very spicy-flavored commercial or favorite recipe barbecue sauce
2 tablespoons crushed dried hot red pepper or crushed dried chile pequin
2 tablespoons chile pasilla (see note) or cayenne pepper
Charro Beans (see index) or grilled corn on the cob (optional)

Place ribs on a rack in a roasting pan large enough to accommodate ribs. Add water. Bake, tightly covered, in a preheated slow oven (325°F.) for 2 hours. Remove ribs, draining well. In a small bowl, combine barbecue sauce, crushed dried red pepper, and chile pasilla, blending well. Arrange ribs on a grill rack, 8 to 10 inches above medium charcoal (ash gray and glowing) in a grill fire box; coat ribs with barbecue sauce and grill for 3 to 4 minutes. Turn ribs and brush with sauce, coating well. Continue to grill for 3 to 4 minutes. Ribs may be slightly charred but not burned. Serve immediately accompanied with Charro Beans or grilled corn on the cob, if desired.

Note: Baby back ribs are the small meaty pork ribs without gristle.
Note: Chile pasilla is a chile pepper or can be found in powdered dried form in specialty food stores. It is not as hot-spiced in flavor as cayenne pepper.

Steak Ranchero
(Grilled Steak with Ranch-style Sauce)
8 servings

This particular carne or steak dish has become one of the most popular at Lista's. Starting out first as a nightly special, it has earned its own place on an already ambitious menu. You will not believe how simple this is to prepare. Serve with your choice of beans and rice. One of my favorite dishes to serve with Steak Ranchero is Papas de la Casa.

Salsa Ranchera (see index)
8 (10 to 12-ounce) beef Delmonico or rib-eye steaks
Garlic powder, to taste
Salt and freshly ground black pepper to taste
Shredded Monterey Jack cheese for garnish as desired (optional)
Papas de la Casa (see index) (optional)

Prepare Salsa Ranchera and keep warm over low heat. Rub *each* steak with garlic powder to taste; sprinkle *each* with salt and pepper as desired. Grill steaks as directed in Beef Tenderloin with Black Bean and Green Chile Salsa (see index). Arrange steaks on heated oven-proof dinner plates; spoon warm Salsa Ranchera as desired over *each*. Sprinkle cheese over *each*, if desired. Accompany with Papas de la Casa, if desired.

The flavor of the chile pepper is fragile and present in the flesh of the chile pod. Since the skins are tough, they should be removed if the chiles are to be used whole. The ribs, seeds, and stems should also be discarded due to their quality of hotness.

Tesoro del Mar
(Treasures of the sea)
8 servings

1 cup lump crabmeat
1 medium green bell pepper, cored, seeded, and chopped
1 medium onion, peeled and chopped
2 tablespoons hot *extra virgin* olive oil
1 tablespoon seafood seasoning (see note)
1 1/2 teaspoons New Mexico-style (bright red) chili powder
8 cups water
2 cups medium (*51 to 60 count*) shrimp, cleaned, deveined, tails removed
2 cups bay scallops
16 mussels (optional)
8 very small (*little neck*) or small (*top neck*) clams (optional)
8 lobster claws (optional)

Pick over crabmeat, removing any shell or cartilage; set aside. In a large stockpot, sauté bell pepper and onion in olive oil until tender. Add seafood seasoning, chili powder, and water; bring to a boil over moderate heat. Add shrimp and scallops; cook for *just* 2 minutes, remove and set aside, covered. Add clams, mussels, and lobster; simmer, cover ajar, *just* until shells open, about 7 to 8 minutes; add cooked shrimp, scallops, and crab-meat, mixing lightly. Serve immediately.

Note: Preferably use Old Bay brand seafood seasoning.

Santa Fe Strip Steak
4 servings

One of my favorite methods of cooking is the old cajun way. I keep experimenting with different combinations of spices to blacken fish or meat. Here is one of Lista's favorites.

1 tablespoon sugar
1 tablespoon paprika
1 tablespoon New Mexico-style (bright red) chili powder
1 tablespoon salt or to taste
1 tablespoon freshly ground black pepper or to taste
1/2 teaspoon ground cumin
1/2 teaspoon dry mustard
1/2 teaspoon dried oregano
1/4 cup *extra virgin* olive oil or butter or margarine
4 (12-ounce) beef strip steaks

In a 1-cup measure, combine the first 8 ingredients, mixing well. Generous-ly rub or pound the spice mixture into both sides of *each* steak. Heat the oil in a large cast-iron skillet over moderate heat to hot (400°F.). Add steaks to skillet and quickly pan-fry (grill), about 2 minutes per side for medium rare, or until desired doneness is achieved. *Do not overcook as beef will lose its flavor and tenderness.*

<hr>

Preparing Chiles

Remember that the skin of chiles is very tough and must be peeled before using in most recipes. Roasting or par-boiling loosens the skin.

To roast and peel: If your hands are not used to acid, use gloves. Select smooth chile pods; arrange pods on a baking sheet and broil 3 to 4 inches from heat source, turning pods frequently as they begin to blister. The entire pod should be charred but not burned. Remove from broiler. Wrap in a clean damp cloth or place in a brown bag or zip-lock plastic bag; allow to steam for 10 minutes.

If you plan to use peppers for Chile Rellenos (Poblano peppers or Anaheim peppers only), leave the stem intact. Slit open one side of the pepper and remove seeds (remember, most of the pepper's flavor is in the seeds). Peel the outer skin downward.

Steak Relleno
(Stuffed Steak)
4 servings

This recipe is tough and I don't mean chewy. You need a nice chorizo sausage. My version may be found on page 48. You may stuff these steaks with just about any-thing, even shrimp, crabmeat, vegetables, or cheese. Be creative! Serve with Frijóles Refritos and Spanish Rice.

4 beef strip steaks, *each* about 8 to 10 ounces, completely trimmed, butterflied (see note), and pounded very thin with a meat mallet (do not make holes in the meat)
8 ounces Chorizo (sausage) (see index)
1 medium green bell pepper, cored, seeded, and cut into thin strips
1 medium firm *ripe* tomato, chopped
1/2 medium onion, peeled thinly sliced and cut into thin strips
4 ounces (1 cup) shredded sharp Cheddar or Monterey Jack cheese, divided
4 slices bacon
Small wooden picks as needed
Salsa Roja or Salsa Ranchera (see index)
Frijóles Refritos (refried beans) (see index)
Spanish Rice (see index)

Prepare steaks for cooking. In a lightly greased large heavy skillet, sauté sausage, pepper, tomato, and onion over moderate heat for 2 to 3 minutes. Lay out steaks and spoon one fourth of the stuffing and one fourth of the cheese onto *each*; fold up sides of *each* steak, then roll jelly roll-style, hold-ing in sides of *each* steak. Wrap *each* relleno with a bacon slice, securing *each* with a wooden pick. In the previously used large heavy skillet, thoroughly brown steaks over moderate heat; reduce heat and simmer, covered, about 10 minutes. To serve, top *each* steak with Salsa Roja or Salsa Ranchera.

Note: To butterfly, slit each steak in half lengthwise with a sharp knife, cutting each almost through. Steaks will open out flat but remain joined at the center.

<hr>

Veal Evangelista
6 servings

Veal Evangelista won raves with Lista's patrons when I introduced it as a special for New Year's Eve. Although the preparation requires some extra effort, you and your guests will appreciate the end result immensely.

6 (6 to 7-ounce) veal cutlets (see note)
1 cup lump crabmeat or cut-up cooked lobster (see note)
2 cups *fresh* broccoli florets
1/2 cup boiling water
1 cup shredded Monterey Jack cheese
1/2 cup minced *fresh* or canned Anaheim mild green chile peppers
Small wooden picks as needed
About 2 tablespoons butter or *extra virgin* olive oil for sautéing
Salsa Blanca (New Mexican Jalapeño Cream Sauce) (see index)
Thinly sliced green onions (scallions) (include some green tops) for garnish
Black Beans 'n Rice (see index)

With a meat mallet or the side of a French knife blade, flatten *each* cutlet, resulting in six thin 8-inch diameter veal slices. Pick over crabmeat, removing any shell or cartilage; set aside. Or, cut cooked lobster meat (tail or claw meat) into bite-size pieces; set aside.

In a medium heavy saucepan, steam broccoli florets on a rack over 1/2 cup boiling water, until *just* tender, about 3 minutes; drain well. Add crabmeat or lobster, cheese, and chile peppers, mixing well. Spoon mixture atop veal cutlets, dividing evenly. Fold the sides of the cutlets inward and then roll *each* tightly, jelly roll-style, securing *each* with wooden picks.

Melt butter or heat oil in a large heavy skillet over moderate heat. Add cutlets and sauté, turning occasionally, until cutlets are browned and tender, about 15 minutes. Arrange *each* cutlet on a heated dinner plate. Spoon about 2 tablespoons New Mexican Jalapeño Cream Sauce atop *each* cutlet and garnish *each* with thinly sliced green onions. Serve with Black Beans n' Rice.

Note: May use chicken or turkey breast cutlets, if desired.

Note: 2 (6-ounce) lobster tails yield about 1 cup cooked lobster meat.

Veal Picado
(Spicy Veal)
4 servings

Veal Picado is a versatile recipe which can be prepared in minutes. The most difficult part of the preparation will be a decision of the choice of accompaniments. Try my Caribe Glazed Carrots or Papas de la Casa as an alternative to beans and rice.

1 pound veal, cut into thin strips, *each* about 1 1/2-inches in length
1/2 cup flour
2 garlic cloves, peeled and minced

1/4 cup hot *extra virgin* olive oil
2 firm *ripe* medium tomatoes, peeled and cut into wedges
2 *fresh* serrano or jalapeño chile peppers, cored, seeded, and cut
    into thin strips
1 medium onion, peeled, and cut into thin vertical strips or wedges
1 medium green bell pepper, cored, seeded, and cut into thin
    strips or wedges
1 medium sweet red bell pepper, cored, seeded, and cut into
    thin strips or wedges
2 teaspoons minced *fresh* or 1 teaspoon dried Mexican oregano
Salt and freshly ground black pepper to taste
3 cups tomato juice
Caribe Glazed Carrots (see index) (optional)
Papas de la Casa (see index) (optional)

On a sheet of wax paper or in a zip-lock plastic bag, dredge veal pieces in
flour, coating *each* lightly. In a large heavy skillet, brown veal in oil over
moderate heat, turning frequently, about 5 minutes. Add garlic while
browning veal. Add vegetables and spices and continue to sauté for 5
minutes, stirring constantly. Add tomato juice; reduce heat and simmer,
covered, for 10 minutes. Serve immediately and accompany with Caribe
Glazed Carrots or Papas de la Casa or a side-dish of choice.

Pollo Borracho
(Drunken Chicken)
4 large or 8 small servings

4 Cornish hens, *each* about 1 pound, or whole chicken breasts
2 tablespoons *extra virgin* olive oil
2 tablespoons minced *fresh* or 1 tablespoon dried rosemary
2 teaspoons minced *fresh* or 1 teaspoon dried oregano
1 teaspoon crushed dried hot red pepper
1 teaspoon garlic powder
1 teaspoon freshly ground black pepper
Salsa Borracho (Drunken Sauce) (see index)

Rinse Cornish hens in cold water; wipe dry with absorbent paper. Tie legs
of hens together with twine; place wings behind backs of hens, turned
akimbo. Rub Cornish hens or chicken breasts (all over) with olive oil.
Sprinkle herbs and spices over *each*, rubbing mixture into *each*. Arrange
hens on a metal rack in a 13 x 9 x 2-inch baking pan or roasting pan. Bake,
uncovered, in a preheated slow oven (325°F.) for 30 minutes. While hens
are baking, prepare Salsa Borracho. Liberally baste hens with sauce and
continue to bake for 20 minutes or until hens are done. Hens or chicken
breasts may be cut in half lengthwise with a sharp knife or kitchen shears.
Arrange a whole or half hen on *each* dinner plate. Garnish as desired. Pass
hot Salsa Borracho in a sauceboat.

Antonio's Spinach Stuffed Pork Roast
4 to 6 servings

At age 18, my son Antonio is another Evangelista with a natural flair for food. He has an ability to combine a few ingredients and produce a finished, almost artistic, culinary masterpiece. One evening he created a marvelous tasting stuffed pork roast. Needless to say, I am very proud of his abilities.

1 (2 to 3-pound) pork tenderloin
1 garlic clove, peeled and chopped
1 cup chopped peeled onion
2 tablespoons hot *extra virgin* olive oil
1 pound spinach, thoroughly cleaned (all sand and grit removed),
    well dried between sheets of absorbent paper, and stems removed
1 tablespoon minced *fresh* or 1 1/2 teaspoons dried cilantro
1 teaspoon minced *fresh* or 1/2 teaspoon dried oregano
Salt and freshly ground black pepper to taste
1 1/2 cups shredded Monterey Jack cheese
Favorite potato recipe or hot cooked rice

With a sharp knife, *very carefully* cut the tenderloin lengthwise along one side, separating the slit outward; *carefully* flatten out tenderloin. Continue to cut, as if peeling an orange and leaving the peel in one piece. Lay tenderloin out on a flat surface. With a meat mallet or the flat side of a French knife, gently pound the tenderloin. *Do not tear.* Set aside.

In a medium heavy skillet, sauté garlic and onion in olive oil over moderate heat for 1 to 2 minutes. *Do not burn.* Add spinach, cilantro, oregano, and salt and pepper to taste; continue to sauté, stirring frequently, for 1 to 2 minutes, until spinach *just* becomes wilted. Drain off any liquid remaining in skillet.

Evenly spread spinach mixture over flattened tenderloin; sprinkle cheese over spinach. Starting at one side, tightly roll roast jelly roll-style, being careful the stuffing does not spill out. Secure with heavy string tied around the roast, spaced in intervals about 3 inches apart. Arrange roast, seam-side down, on a metal rack in a roasting pan. Sprinkle stuffed tenderloin with salt and pepper as desired. Bake, uncovered, in a preheated slow oven (325°F.) for 1 hour. Allow tenderloin to stand for a few minutes to achieve easier carving. With a sharp knife, cut tenderloin into slices. Discard string. Accompany with a favorite potato recipe or hot cooked rice.

Crab Cakes Lista
8 servings

The secret to these little gems is not what you put in them as much as what you leave out. I have found the best tasting crab cakes to be ones which are simply prepared with good quality fresh crabmeat. Of course at Lista's we add just a hint of fire!

2 pounds lump crabmeat
4 large eggs
1 jalapeño or serrano chile pepper, minced

2 cups *fine* cracker crumbs
1/2 cup mayonnaise
1 tablespoon prepared mustard (see note)
1 teaspoon paprika
1 teaspoon seafood seasoning (see note)
2 to 3 tablespoons hot *extra virgin* olive oil (optional)
2 cups Fresh Pineapple and Jalapeño Salsa (see index) at room
    temperature

Pick over crabmeat, carefully removing any shell or cartilage. Be careful
not to breakup crabmeat. Set aside. In a large bowl, combine the next 7 ingredients, mixing well into a smooth paste. Gently fold in crabmeat,
mixing only as required to evenly distribute crabmeat. Form mixture into 8
equal-size thick patties. Pan-fry crab cakes in olive oil in a large heavy skillet over moderate heat until lightly browned and heated through, about 2
to 3 minutes per side. Or, arrange crab cakes on a rack in a broiler pan;
broil, 6 to 8 inches from heat source, about 2 to 3 minutes per side until
lightly browned. Serve immediately, accompanied with Fresh Pineapple
and Jalapeño Salsa.

Note: Preferably use Old Bay brand seafood seasoning.

Gary's Sage Pork with Jalapeño Apricot Salsa
4 to 6 servings

*This zesty main dish recipe was designed by one of my great staff members who
shares the same passion for chile peppers as the Evangelista family.*

2 pounds *very* lean pork tenderloin
2 cups Salsa Verde (see index)
1/4 cup *extra virgin* olive oil
1 tablespoon minced *fresh* or 1 1/2 teaspoons dried sage
1 tablespoon freshly ground black pepper or to taste
1 tablespoon granulated dried garlic or 3 to 4 garlic cloves,
    peeled and minced
1 teaspoon salt or to taste
Jalapeño Apricot Salsa (see index)
Black Bean n' Rice (see index)

With a sharp knife, cut pork tenderloin into 8 (4-ounce) medallions. With a
meat mallet, pound *each* lightly. In a large heavy cast-iron or other heavy
skillet, heat olive oil to about medium (300°F.). In a medium bowl, combine spices, mixing lightly. Coat *each* piece of pork, both sides with spice
mixture. Pan-fry medallions in hot olive oil over low to moderate heat,
about 2 minutes per side. Arrange 1 1/2 to 2 medallions on *each* plate.
Ladle about 1/2 cup Salsa Verde over *each* serving. Accompany with
Jalapeño Apricot Salsa and Black Beans n' Rice.

Ribs Sobrino

(Nephew's Country-style Pork Ribs)
4 to 6 servings

Lista's has been blessed with creative assistant chefs during the past decade. One of the most talented of apprentices has been my nephew, Andrew Evangelista.

5 to 7 pounds country-style pork ribs
About 1 teaspoon salt or to taste
About 1 teaspoon freshly ground black pepper or to taste
About 1 teaspoon garlic powder or to taste
About 4 to 5 cups water
4 cups Chilpotle Pepper Sauce (see index)
4 cups Spanish Rice (see index)
3 cups cooked black beans
1/4 cup minced *fresh* or 3 tablespoons dried, divided, for garnish

Place ribs in a large roasting pan large enough to cover with aluminum foil without touching the ribs. Sprinkle ribs with salt, pepper, and garlic powder as desired. Add water to pan; cover roaster with aluminum foil, being careful not to touch ribs. Bake in a preheated slow oven (325°F.) for 1 1/2 hours.

Drain liquid from ribs. Add Chilpotle Pepper Sauce, coating ribs well. Cover again and continue to bake for 30 minutes. Serve hot ribs over rice accompanied with cooked black beans. Garnish ribs with a sprinkle of cilantro.

Cactus got your tongue!???

Out west, the flat pods of the prickly pear cactus — called nopales — are considered a delicacy. Of course people pull out the needles first and then boil them for use in salsas. The taste is something similar to green beans or okra, nothing like pin cushions!

Aduvada Sauce
about 4 cups

Aduvada Sauce is Lista's version of a spicy BBQ sauce — and I mean spicy! We do our famous hot baby back ribs with this succulent rich sauce.

1/2 cup New Mexico–style (bright red) chili powder
1/3 cup sugar
1/4 cup ancho-style (dark) chili powder
2 tablespoons crushed dried hot red pepper or dried chile pequin
1 tablespoon cayenne pepper
2 teaspoons salt or to taste
1 teaspoon ground cumin
1 teaspoon curry powder
1 teaspoon white pepper or to taste
1 1/2 cups tomato juice
1 cup honey
1/4 cup salad oil
1 tablespoon minced peeled garlic
2 tablespoons cider vinegar
1 tablespoon liquid smoke

In a deep medium bowl, combine the first 9 ingredients, mixing well. In a 4-cup measure, combine the remaining ingredients, blending well. With a wire whisk, blend the tomato juice mixture into the spice mixture, whisking until mixture is smooth and without any lumps. Store Aduvada Sauce, covered, in an airtight container in the refrigerator for up to 14 days.

Avocado Sauce
4 cups

Avocado Sauce is perfect with hot Taquitos or serve as an unusual dip with freshly made corn or flour chips as dippers.

2 *ripe* avocados, peeled, halved, seeds removed, and immediately
  sprinkled with lemon juice
1 jalapeño chile pepper, (including seeds) or 1 teaspoon jalapeño
  chile pepper powder (see note)
2 cups green tomatillos (see note)
1/4 teaspoon ground cumin
1 teaspoon salt or to taste
Water as needed

Combine all ingredients together in a blender container; cover and blend at high speed until mixture is smooth. Add water as needed if mixture is too thick, a small amount at a time, until sauce is medium thick in consistency.

Note: Jalapeño chile pepper powder is available in specialty food markets.
Note: Husks and sticky residue need to be removed. Round vegetables, the size of cherry tomatoes, they are available in the produce section of many grocery stores.

Avocado Relish
4 to 5 servings

I prepare this sauce the same way as the Pico de Gallo sauce, except I add the avocado. Try this with your favorite grilled or charbroiled steak.

4 serrano chile peppers, thinly sliced (optional)
2 *ripe* medium avocados, peeled, seeded, and chopped
2 cups chopped firm *ripe* tomatoes
2 cups chopped peeled onion
2 tablespoons minced *fresh* cilantro (see note)
4 teaspoons *fresh* lime juice
2 teaspoons salt or to taste
1 teaspoon sugar
1/2 teaspoon freshly ground black pepper or to taste

In a medium bowl, combine all ingredients, mixing gently. Cover and chill in the refrigerator for at least 1 hour.

Note: If the relish is being served with roast lamb or other lamb recipes, substitute 1 tablespoon chopped fresh mint leaves for 1 tablespoon chopped cilantro leaves.

Black Bean and Green Chile Salsa
4 cups

Here is another quick, easy to prepare salsa. It is very versatile and lends itself well to beef, pork, chicken, and even seafood.

8 ounces Anaheim mild green chile peppers, roasted and peeled
2 tablespoons *extra virgin* olive oil
1 medium onion, peeled and chopped
1 tablespoon minced peeled garlic
1 teaspoon minced *fresh* or 1/2 teaspoon dried oregano
1 teaspoon minced *fresh* or 1/2 teaspoon dried rosemary
1 teaspoon crushed dried chile pequin or hot red pepper (see note)
2 cups undrained canned black beans or 1 undiluted (16-ounce)
  can black bean soup
About 1 cup water

Arrange green chiles on a rack in a broiler pan; broil, 3 to 4 inches from heat source, until charred on all sides. Remove and place in a paper bag or wrap in wet absorbent paper, closing tightly; allow to stand for 25 to 30 minutes. Peel may be easily removed. With a sharp knife, chop peppers. While peppers are standing, heat olive oil in a medium heavy saucepan over moderate heat. Add onion, garlic, oregano, rosemary, and chile pequin; sauté mixture, stirring frequently, until onion is tender but not browned. Add beans and chopped roasted chiles, mixing well. Bring mixture to a simmer; reduce heat and continue to simmer, uncovered, for 10 minutes. Add water as necessary to achieve desired consistency, blending well.

Note: Available in most specialty food stores.

Chile peppers today are thought to have medicinal powers of lowering blood pressure and blood cholesterol and relieving symptoms of certain types of allergies.

Camarón Sauce
(Shrimp Sauce)
about 2 cups

I use this sauce to coat baked or broiled jumbo shrimp or lobster tails. The aroma will fill your kitchen. Have some Lista's Guacamole or Quesadillas ready when you start.

1 1/2 cups orange juice
1/2 cup *extra virgin* olive oil
1/4 cup *fresh* lemon juice
2 tablespoons minced *fresh* or 1 tablespoon dried cilantro
2 tablespoons minced *fresh* parsley
2 tablespoons chopped peeled garlic
2 tablespoons crushed dried hot red pepper or chile pequin or to taste
1 1/2 teaspoons minced *fresh* or 1/2 to 3/4 teaspoon dried tarragon
1 tablespoon celery salt
1 tablespoon minced *fresh* or 1 1/2 teaspoons dried oregano

Combine all ingredients in a blender container; cover and blend at high speed for about 30 seconds.

Carnitas Relish
(Relish to Accompany Meat)
about 4 cups

2 *ripe* medium avocados, peeled, seeded, and chopped
2 tablespoons *fresh* lime juice
2 firm *ripe* tomatoes, chopped
1 small onion, peeled and chopped
2 tablespoons minced *fresh* cilantro
Pinch of minced *fresh* oregano
Pinch of ground cumin
1 teaspoon salt or to taste
1 teaspoon white pepper or to taste

Prepare avocados; immediately place in a large bowl and evenly sprinkle with lime juice to prevent discoloration of avocados. Add remaining ingredients, mixing gently. Cover and refrigerate for several hours to allow the flavors to blend.

Chilpotle Pepper Sauce
4 servings

This sauce holds and reheats very well.

2 tablespoons *extra virgin* olive oil
2 sweet red bell peppers, cored, seeded, and chopped
1 large onion, peeled and chopped
1 (4-ounce) can chilpotle chile peppers, minced
1 (26-ounce) can tomatoes, crushed (include liquid)
2 tablespoons sugar
1 teaspoon minced *fresh* or 1/2 teaspoon dried rosemary
1/2 teaspoon minced *fresh* or 1/4 teaspoon dried oregano

In a medium heavy saucepan, heat olive oil over moderate heat; add peppers and onion. Sauté, stirring frequently, until vegetables are tender but not browned. Add remaining ingredients and bring mixture to a boil. Reduce heat and simmer, uncovered, for 15 minutes.

Corn Salsa
(Corn Relish)
about 7 cups

4 soft corn tortillas
6 cups whole-kernel corn, freshly cut from the cob, or frozen or
   canned, drained
1 garlic clove, peeled and minced
1 chilpotle chile pepper, *fresh* or canned
2 cups minced peeled onion
1/4 cup minced *fresh* or 2 tablespoons dried cilantro
2 teaspoons minced *fresh* or 1 teaspoon dried oregano
1 teaspoon *fresh* lime juice
1 teaspoon ground cumin
1 teaspoon freshly ground black pepper or to taste
Salt to taste
4 leaves crisp leaf lettuce for garnish
1 firm *ripe* medium tomato, cut into wedges, for garnish
Crisp corn and/or flour chips for dipping

In a food processor or blender container, combine tortillas and corn; cover and process or blend until mixture is finely chopped. *Do not liquify or over-blend or over-process.* Transfer mixture to a large bowl; add garlic, chilpotle chile pepper, onion, cilantro, oregano, lime juice, cumin, black pepper, and salt, mixing well by hand. Cover and chill in the refrigerator for at least 30 minutes. Arrange lettuce leaves in a serving bowl (around the edge). Spoon salsa into the lettuce-lined bowl and garnish with tomato wedges. Accompany with crisp corn and/or flour chips as dippers, if desired.

Extra Extra Hot
about 1 1/2 cups

This sauce is one of our quick blender sauces that will quiet the mouth of your hot-test pepper-eating friend. Everyone has at least one. We use a certain type of canned, hot, peeled pepper, not pickled, processed by Old El Paso or Ortega Foods. Add a variation and you'll have a beautiful bright table sauce.

1 cup whole jalapeño chile peppers, roasted and peeled
  (see directions, page73 or 81)
1 cup water
1/4 cup chopped peeled onion
1 teaspoon salt or to taste
1 teaspoon garlic powder

Combine all ingredients in a blender container; cover and blend at high speed for about 2 minutes.

Variation: Add 1/4 cup chopped peeled onion, 1/4 cup chopped peeled tomato, and 1 1/2 teaspoons minced fresh cilantro, mixing lightly.

Fresh Pineapple and Jalapeño Salsa
about 4 cups

1 *ripe* large pineapple, peeled, cored, and cut into large pieces
1/2 *fresh* jalapeño chile pepper
1 tablespoon *fresh* lemon juice
1 tablespoon *fresh* lime juice
1 tablespoon minced *fresh* or 1 1/2 teaspoons dried cilantro
1/2 teaspoon minced peeled garlic
1/2 teaspoon ground cumin

Combine pineapple and jalapeño chile pepper in a food processor or blender container; cover and process or blend until both are minced but not puréed (see note). Add remaining ingredients by hand, mixing lightly. Chill if desired. Serve chilled or at room temperature.

Note: If food processor is not available, chop pineapple and jalapeño chile pepper medium fine with a French knife.

Green Chile Chutney
about 3 cups

Green Chile Chutney is easy to prepare and has many uses. Its versatility is the key. The flavor blends well with eggs. Here at Lista's, we've served Green Chile Chutney with crab or salmon cakes, roast pork, and chicken.

2 pounds New Mexico or Anaheim mild green chile peppers, roasted
  and peeled (see directions page 73, or 81), and chopped
1 cup sugar

1/2 cup cider vinegar
1 tablespoon minced *fresh* or 1 1/2 teaspoons dried oregano
1 teaspoon salt or to taste
Pinch of ground cumin

In a medium heavy saucepan, combine all ingredients; cook, stirring occasionally, over low heat for 12 to 15 minutes. Allow to cool. Serve cold.

Note: For a spicier flavored chutney, add 2 chopped, peeled, roasted fresh jalapeño chile peppers. See page 73 or 81 for directions.

Lemon Tequila Sauce
2 cups

Lemon Tequila Sauce complements the Santa Fe Bread Pudding but may be used for other recipes as desired.

2 eggs, lightly beaten
1/2 cup sugar
1/4 cup butter or margarine, melted
1/4 cup tequila
2 tablespoons *fresh* lemon juice

In a small heavy saucepan, combine all ingredients, mixing well. Stir over moderate heat until mixture *just* comes to a simmer. *Do not boil.*

Lista's Enchilada Sauce
1 quart

Over the past decade or so, Lista's has been known for its enchiladas. Below is a quick version of our famous sauce.

2 teaspoons cooking oil
1/4 cup New Mexico-style (bright red) chili powder
2 teaspoons salt or to taste
2 teaspoons sugar
1/4 teaspoon garlic powder
3 cups hot water
1/2 cup flour
2/3 cup cold water

In a large heavy saucepan, heat oil to medium (350°F.) over moderate heat. With a wire whisk, blend in chili powder; stir mixture over heat for about 2 minutes, until mixture is smooth. Add salt, sugar, and garlic powder. Blend in hot water. Bring mixture to a brisk boil; reduce heat and allow to cool slightly, about 5 minutes. In a small bowl, blend cold water into the flour with a wire whisk, dissolving all lumps. Strain flour-water mixture. Gradually blend flour mixture into the hot enchilada sauce, stirring constantly. Allow sauce to simmer, uncovered, for an additional 10 to 14 minutes, stirring occasionally.

Lista's Hot Sauce
(Table Sauce)
about 6 1/2 cups

Throughout this book, I refer to hot sauce because it has many uses and goes with many recipes. It's marvelous as a chilled sauce for dipping crisp tortilla chips, as well as served warm over eggs for Huevos Rancheros or over grilled (beef steak) Carne Asada. Some folks like it spooned over their favorite burritos with a bit of cheese garnish. Once you've prepared the sauce a few times, you'll find more and more uses for it.

1 garlic clove, peeled and minced
4 cups chopped firm *ripe* tomatoes
2 cups cold water
1/2 cup chopped peeled onion
1/4 cup minced jalapeño chile peppers
2 teaspoons minced *fresh* or 1 teaspoon dried cilantro
1 teaspoon minced *fresh* or 1/2 teaspoon dried oregano
1/2 teaspoon ground cumin
Salt and freshly ground black pepper to taste

In a large bowl, combine the first 9 ingredients. Add salt and pepper to taste, mixing well. Cover and refrigerate until thoroughly chilled. Serve cold as desired. Or, simmer sauce, uncovered, in a large heavy saucepan over moderate heat, stirring frequently, for 5 minutes. (The flavor will be changed, but the sauce will retain a *fresh*-cut flavor.)

Lista's Special Cocktail Sauce
about 3 cups

1 3/4 cups catsup
3/4 cup cold water
3 tablespoons grated peeled horseradish root
2 tablespoons *fresh* lemon juice
1 1/2 tablespoons minced *fresh* parsley
1 teaspoon Worcestershire Sauce
1 teaspoon Tabasco sauce
1 1/2 teaspoons minced *fresh* cilantro

In a small bowl, combine all ingredients, beating lightly with a wire whisk, blending well. Store, covered, in an airtight container in the refrigerator for up to 10 days.

Mexican Brunch Hollandaise Sauce
2 cups

Mexican-style Hollandaise Sauce is perfect over your favorite omelettes or Eggs Benedict. It complements any fresh steamed vegetable.

1 cup butter or margarine
2 (.9 ounce) packages Hollandaise Sauce mix (see note)
1/4 cup chopped green or sweet red bell pepper
1 tablespoon minced jalapeño chile peppers
1/2 teaspoon freshly ground black pepper or to taste
1/2 teaspoon cayenne pepper or to taste
Pinch of minced *fresh* cilantro
2 cups milk

In a medium heavy saucepan, melt butter over low heat. With a wire whisk, add Hollandaise Sauce mix, blending well. Add bell and jalapeño peppers, black and cayenne peppers, and cilantro. Gradually add milk, blending well. Increase heat to moderate; cook, stirring constantly, until sauce is smooth and thickened. Use immediately or keep warm, covered, in the top of a double boiler over simmering water. *Do not keep warm over direct heat source as sauce may curdle.*

Note: Preferably use Knorr brand Hollandaise Sauce mix.

Peach Salsa
(Peach Relish)
2 cups

This salsa is one of the newest in my repertoire. It can be served hot or chilled. I first created it for a Cerdo Relleno (stuffed pork) Lista's recently featured. Because of its popularity, it probably will be served often.

3 firm *ripe* large peaches, peeled, *each* cut in half, and seeds removed
2 tablespoons butter or margarine
1/4 cup chopped sweet red bell pepper
1 teaspoon minced serrano chile pepper
1 tablespoon *fresh* lime juice
2 tablespoons peach brandy

With a sharp knife, chop peaches into small pieces. In a medium heavy skillet, melt butter over low heat. Add peaches, sweet red pepper, and serrano pepper; increase heat and sauté until *just* tender. Add lime juice, mixing gently. Add peach brandy and ignite. When flame has burned out, immediately serve, or cool and chill, covered, in refrigerator for up to 7 days.

Molé Rojo
(Spicy Red Sauce with Chocolate)
3 cups

10 dried ancho chile peppers, ground
8 dried negro or dried pasilla chile peppers, ground
6 dried mulato or dried poblano chile peppers, ground
6 firm *ripe* Italian-style pear shaped tomatoes
4 garlic cloves, peeled and chopped
2 squares (ounces) unsweetened chocolate
1/2 cup lightly salted peanuts
1/2 cup dark seedless raisins
1/3 cup sesame seeds
2 teaspoons cinnamon
4 cups water
2 cups chicken broth or stock (see note)
1 tablespoon peanut oil

Combine one half of *each* of the first 11 ingredients in a food processor or blender container; cover and process or blend at high speed until ingredients become a smooth paste. Transfer mixture to a 2-quart heavy saucepan or stockpot. Repeat process with the remaining amounts of the first 11 ingredients and add to mixture in the saucepan. Add water, chicken broth, and peanut oil, mixing well. Bring to a simmer over moderate heat; continue to simmer, uncovered, for 15 minutes, stirring occasionally. *Do not allow sauce to boil.* Use with favorite poultry. Sauce may be stored in an airtight container in the refrigerator for up to 4 days.

Note: 1 1/2 undiluted (10 1/2-ounce) cans chicken broth may be substituted for homemade chicken broth or stock.

Pico de Gallo
(Classic Mexican-style Relish)
about 4 cups

This is one of the staples of zesty southwestern and New Mexican-style cooking. The only true rule to Pico is that it must be fresh! Be creative with this salsa. It goes well with just about everything from your favorite fajitas to grilled fish — even roasted poultry. The more you use Pico, the more you'll love it.

4 serrano chile peppers, thinly sliced
2 cups chopped firm *ripe* tomatoes
2 cups chopped peeled onion
2 tablespoons minced *fresh* cilantro
2 teaspoons *fresh* lime juice
2 teaspoons salt or to taste
1 teaspoon sugar
1/2 teaspoon freshly ground black pepper or to taste

In a medium bowl, combine all ingredients, mixing gently. Chill, covered, in the refrigerator for at least 30 minutes before serving.

Salsa Ananás
(Spicy Pineapple Sauce)
4 cups

We first put this sauce together for Crab Cakes Lista's and salmon cakes. It adds an exciting taste to seafood.

1 *very ripe* pineapple, cored, peeled, and cut into medium pieces
1 jalapeño chile pepper, minced
2 tablespoons *fresh* lemon juice
1 tablespoon dry white wine
Pinch of minced peeled garlic

Combine all ingredients in a food processor or blender container; cover and process or blend until mixture is a coarse purée. Serve warm or chilled as a side-dish or relish.

Salsa Borracho
(Drunken Sauce)
4 cups

This sauce is a popular one we did a few years ago to serve over roasted Cornish hens or small chickens. It is also an excellent addition to lean pork.

3 cups orange juice
2 cups honey
1 cup *extra virgin* olive oil
1/2 cup dark rum
2 tablespoons paprika
2 tablespoons crushed dried hot red pepper or crushed dried chile pequin
2 tablespoons chopped peeled garlic
1 tablespoon minced *fresh* or 1 1/2 teaspoons dried rosemary
1 tablespoon minced *fresh* or 1 1/2 teaspoons dried oregano
1 tablespoon freshly ground black pepper or to taste

In a 2-quart heavy saucepan, combine all ingredients; bring to a light boil over moderate heat. Store in an airtight container, tightly covered, in the refrigerator for up to 7 days.

Salsa Fresca
(Fresh Raw Vegetable Sauce)
about 2 cups

Fresh is the key ingredient to Salsa Fresca. Although it tastes marvelous, this salsa does not keep well. Prepare just enough for the meal for which it is to be served. I use it mostly as a garnish for steaks or fish or pork — the carnitas. This salsa is similar to Pico de Gallo; however, it is somewhat more mild in flavor and different in consistency.

2 firm *ripe large* tomatoes, peeled and chopped
2 *fresh* jalapeño or serrano chile peppers, minced
1 large onion, peeled and chopped
2 tablespoons *fresh* lime juice
2 tablespoons minced *fresh* or 1 tablespoon dried cilantro
1 teaspoon cider vinegar
Salt and freshly ground black pepper

In a small bowl, combine the first 6 ingredients, mixing gently. Or, place all ingedients in a blender container; cover and chop *very* fine on medium speed. Season with salt and pepper to taste.

Salsa Naranja
(Orange Sauce)
4 cups

My favorite entree to serve with this sauce is flounder or other fresh whitefish.

2 tablespoons *extra virgin* olive oil
2 garlic cloves, peeled and minced
1 large onion, peeled and cut into thin strips
3 ounces chilpotle chile peppers in Adobo Sauce, minced (see note)
3 tablespoons corn starch
1 cup cold water
3 cups orange juice
1/4 cup sugar

In a medium heavy saucepan, heat oil over moderate heat; add garlic and onion. Sauté, stirring frequently, until onion is tender but not browned. Add peppers; continue to sauté, stirring frequently, for 2 minutes. In a small bowl, blend cold water into corn starch, blending until mixture is smooth. Gradually stir corn starch mixture into pepper mixture. Add orange juice and sugar, blending well. Bring mixture to a light boil, stirring constantly.

Note: Available in most specialty food stores.

Salsa Ranchera
(Ranch-stye Sauce)
6 cups

We just call this ranch-style sauce Salsa Ranchera because it has become so popular with our patrons. In the Southwest, ranch-style refers to simple foods, etc. One of my most versatile sauces, it also happens to be one of the most simple to prepare. Don't tell your guests and I won't tell anyone but you!

2 tablespoons *extra virgin* olive oil
4 firm *ripe* tomatoes, cut into wedges
2 medium green bell peppers, cored, seeded, and cut into thin strips
2 garlic cloves, peeled and minced
1 large white onion, peeled, thinly sliced, and cut into strips
4 (6-ounce) cans tomato juice
2 jalapeño chile peppers, chopped (for a milder sauce, remove seeds)
Pinch of minced *fresh* cilantro (optional)
Pinch of minced *fresh* oregano
Salt and pepper to taste

In a large heavy saucepan, heat oil to medium (350°F.) over moderate heat; add tomatoes, green pepper, garlic, and onion. Sauté, stirring frequently, *until vegetables are tender, but not soggy or limp.* Add tomato juice and bring mixture to a boil. Add herbs; season with salt and pepper to taste. Immediately remove from heat. Sauce may be stored in an airtight container, covered, in the refrigerator for up to 4 to 5 days.

Salsa Verde
(Green Chile Sauce)
about 2 cups

Salsa Verde is probably the most versatile sauce in New Mexican-style cooking. It goes well with the simple taste of fried eggs and potatoes — the basic New Mexican-style breakfast. It enhances the taste of poultry and does something wonderful to the flavor of fish.

4 cups New Mexico green chile peppers, roasted, peeled, stems removed
    (see page 73, or 81), and chopped
6 to 8 garlic cloves, peeled and minced
1/2 cup chopped peeled onion
2 teaspoons salt or to taste
2 teaspoons minced *fresh* or 1 teaspoon ground dried Mexican oregano
1 teaspoon ground cumin

Prepare peppers. In a blender container, combine all ingredients; cover and blend until mixture is chopped. *Do not purée.* Store in a tightly covered container in the refrigerator for up to 8 to 10 days. To serve, warm sauce in a heavy saucepan of choice over low heat. Use with a variety of recipes.

Jalapeño Apricot Salsa
4 to 5 servings

Many poultry and pork recipes lend themselves to a sweet side-dish. Although I prefer Jalapeño Apricot Salsa as the recipe is given, it also can be made by chopping the jalapeños and apricots into small pieces.

2 tablespoons butter or margarine, melted
1 large jalapeño chile pepper, cut into *very* thin strips
1 (16-ounce) can apricot halves, drained
Pinch of nutmeg
Pinch of cinnamon
1/4 cup shelled piñóns (pinenuts) or peanuts (optional)
Gary's Sage Pork or Pollo Borracho (optional) (see index)

In a large non-stick skillet, melt butter over moderate heat. Add jalapeño and quickly sauté for 10 to 15 seconds, stirring constantly. Add apricots, increase heat, and continue to sauté, about 5 to 6 minutes, *shaking and carefully turning appricots to allow apricot halves to remain whole and not become mushy.* Serve hot or at room temperature. Sprinkle with pinenuts or peanuts *just* before serving. Serve as a side dish with Gary's Sage Pork or Pollo Borracho, if desired.

Chili or Chile ?

"It's a muddled word, spelled at least three ways (chili, chile, chilli) and with at least three different meanings: it is the edible fruit of a genus of plants called Capsicum; it is a dried spice; and it is a hot stew. Christopher Columbus mistook Hispaniolan capsicums for a form of black-pepper plant and named them accordingly, resulting in chili peppers having a dubious identity. Even experts aren't clear about what they are: botanists think of them as a berry of the nightshade family, such as the tomato; horticulturists consider them a fruit; New Mexico, where nearly everybody spells it with an "e," has declared it an official state vegetable."

"As a spice, it has played a big role only in regional cooking, such as the piquant fare of Creole, Cajun, and Tex-Mex kitchens, and that of the descendants of Spanish settlers in St. Augustine, Florida, who incorporate the blazing datil chili into seafood chowders and casseroles."

"As an edible fruit, chile has a reputation that has changed dramatically in recent years. Chile peppers have become a popular symbol of chic Southwestern style."

"Chiles are the key to the recent great success of fajitas and burritos as franchised food, and of spicy chicken wings and nachos — all of which have become nearly as common as hamburgers and hot dogs. There isn't a supermarket or gourmet shop from East to West coast that doesn't have at least a small selection of once unusual chile pepper-based sauces, seasonings, and condiments."

LEGUMBRES
Y
ENSALADAS

Legumbres (Vegetables)

Most Mexican-style restaurants throughout the United States offer very little in vegetables. For myself, I can't get enough of them and I keep trying different methods of preparation in an effort to make them more interesting to diners. The next few pages detail some of Lista's favorites. Just about anything goes together, serve a favorite meat, fish, or poultry recipe with a zesty vegetable dish. Of course, fresh vegetables have no substitute for flavor; however, ease, convenience, and speed of preparation are very important considerations. Some good frozen and canned vegetables products are available and worthy of use in many recipes.

Black Beans n' Rice
4 to 6 servings

2 cups dried black beans
About 8 cups water
1/2 cup *extra virgin* olive oil
1 tablespoon salt or to taste
1 teaspoon minced *fresh* or 1/2 teaspoon dried oregano
1 teaspoon ground cumin
1 teaspoon freshly ground black pepper or to taste
4 to 6 cups cooked long-grain white rice (optional)
About 1 to 1 1/2 cups chopped peeled onion for garnish, divided

Carefully pick over beans, removing any foreign objects. Rinse beans twice in cold water, draining well. In a 2-quart heavy saucepan or stockpot, combine beans and remaining ingredients except rice and onions; bring to a boil over high heat, stirring occasionally. Continue to boil, partially covered for 30 minutes. Add additional water as necessary. Reduce heat and simmer, partially covered, for 1 1/2 hours or until beans are tender (see note). Spoon beans into bowls or onto plates, dividing evenly. May spoon beans over individual servings of cooked rice, about 1/4 cup, if desired. Garnish *each* serving with chopped onions.

Note: Some people prefer black beans slightly firm, others like them cooked to an almost mushy consistency. Adjust cooking time to desired preference of beans. This recipe provides cooked beans with a slightly firm texture and consistency.

Calabacitas
(Sautéed Corn and Zucchini with Peppers)
4 servings

Calabacitas is a classic New Mexican side-dish which is an excellent accompaniment for pork chops or Carne Aduvada. It is simple and quick to prepare. I'm sure you'll find many entrees with which to serve this tasty vegetable dish.

2 cups *fresh* whole-kernel corn, freshly cut from the cob
3 tablespoons hot *extra virgin* olive oil, or butter or margarine,   melted
2 cups sliced unpeeled zucchini squash

1/2 teaspoon minced peeled garlic
2 *fresh* Anaheim mild chile peppers or 1 jalapeño chile pepper, stems removed and minced
Salt and freshly ground black pepper to taste

In a large heavy skillet, sauté corn in oil over moderate heat for 4 to 5 minutes, stirring frequently. Add zucchini and garlic, mixing well. Reduce heat and add chile peppers and salt and pepper to taste. Cook, uncovered, 4 to 5 minutes, stirring frequently. Serve immediately.

Mom's Cauliflower
4 to 6 servings

I remember quite well the evening meals that my mother would prepare when I was a child. Because my father was a true chef, we always wanted him to do the cooking, however, there were times my mom would step in to cook even though dad's shoes were hard to fill. She prepared some wonderful tasty dishes that required little preparation. Her cauliflower was one such side-dish that would accompany pan-fried pork chops or crispy fried fresh water trout.

1 large head cauliflower, leaves and core removed, cut into florets
2 cups water
3/4 cup flour
1 tablespoon butter or margarine
1 teaspoon freshly ground black pepper
Salt to taste
3 cups milk

In a 4-quart heavy saucepan, combine cauliflower and water; bring to a quick boil over high heat. Cover tightly and remove from heat; set aside.

In 2-quart heavy saucepan, brown the flour over low heat, about 2 to 3 minutes, stirring constantly. Add remaining ingredients except cauliflower and milk, stirring quickly with a wire whisk. *Do not allow mixture to form lumps.* Gradually add milk. Increase heat to moderate and continue cooking, whisking constantly, until sauce is thickened and bubbly hot.

Drain water completely from cauliflower, fold vegetable into cooked sauce. Adjust seasonings. Serve immediately.

Variation: Add a few peeled carrot slices to the cauliflower during the cooking process.

We're Jumping With Beans!!!

Did you know that beans are practically a perfect food? They contain more protein than any other plant food. They're also rich in fiber and complex carbohydrates. Nutritionists love beans and so do we. We season ours with fresh peppers, chiles, and spices to make a naturally healthy food delicious.

Charro Beans
(Pinto Beans Seasoned with Spicy Sausage and Cilantro)
6 servings

A small pot of Charro Beans is another side-dish that is served with all our fajitas and many of our special entrees of the evening. We add a couple of extra ingredients to our regular pinto beans — that's the easy part — the hard part is keeping up with the demand for them.

4 cups Frijóles de Olla (see index)
4 ounces cooked Chorizo (sausage), crumbled (see index)
1/4 cup chopped peeled onion
1/4 cup chile caribe or 1 tablespoon crushed dried hot red pepper
1 tablespoon minced *fresh* or 1 1/2 teaspoons dried cilantro

Prepare Frijóles de Olla and Chorizo in advance. Combine beans, sausage, and remaining ingredients in a medium heavy saucepan. Bring to a simmer over low heat; continue to simmer, uncovered, for 10 minutes. Serve immediately.

Caribe Glazed Carrots
(Spicy Glazed Carrots)
4 to 6 servings

2 pounds carrots, peeled, *each* cut lengthwise in half, and then
   cut into 2-inch pieces
4 cups water
1/2 cup honey
1/4 cup chile caribe or cayene pepper to taste
2 tablespoons butter or margarine, at room temperature
1/2 teaspoon ground cumin

In a large heavy saucepan, bring water to a brisk boil over high heat; add carrots, reduce heat to moderate, and cook, covered, until carrots are *just* tender, about 10 to 15 minutes. Drain well. Add remaining ingredients to carrots in saucepan, mixing lightly. Return pan to low heat and continue to cook, uncovered, stirring frequently, for 3 to 5 minutes. *Do not overcook; carrots should not be too soft or mushy.* Serve immediately as a side-dish.

Chilpotle Pepper Squash
4 servings

Chilpotle peppers are a must in the preparation of this recipe. Use fresh, dried, or canned — whichever is available.

1/4 medium onion, peeled and cut into thin strips
2 tablespoons hot *extra virgin* olive oil
1 pound zucchini or yellow (summer) squash, thinly sliced
1 firm *ripe* medium tomato, peeled and chopped
1 garlic clove, peeled and minced
2 tablespoons minced chilpotle chile peppers (see note)
1 tablespoon minced *fresh* cilantro or parsley
1/2 teaspoon minced *fresh* or 1/4 teaspoon dried oregano

In a large heavy skillet, sauté onion in olive oil over moderate heat for 2 minutes, stirring frequently. Add zucchini or yellow squash, tomato, and garlic; continue to cook, stirring frequently, until vegetables are *tender but not mushy*, about 2 minutes. Add peppers, cilantro, and oregano; continue to cook for 1 minute. *Do not overcook.* Serve as a side-dish to accompany an entree of choice.

Frijóles de Olla
(Pinto Beans in a Pot)
8 servings

I grew up in a Mexican household where beans were served once a day, just as in my wife Kathy's Irish family, potatoes were always served. Our mothers would start cooking the beans or potatoes without thinking about what they were doing, then say to themselves, "What do I fix for dinner?" Naturally, everyone in our family expected beans to be served at the main meal.

1 pound dried pinto beans
Water as needed
1 tablespoon plus 1 1/2 teaspoons salt or to taste
1 tablespoon plus 1 1/2 teaspoons New Mexico-style (bright red)
   chili powder
1 tablespoon freshly ground black pepper or to taste
1 tablespoon granulated dried garlic or 3 to 4 garlic cloves,
   peeled and minced
1/4 cup peanut or other cooking oil

Sort through dried beans, removing any foreign objects; rinse beans thoroughly and place in a large bowl. Add cold water to cover well. Allow beans to stand for 12 hours at room temperature; drain well. Place beans in a large heavy stockpot; add 10 cups water and remaining ingredients. Cook, uncovered, over moderate heat for 2 hours, checking the amount of liquid occasionally. Add water as necessary if consistency of the beans begins to look too thick; liquid should remain slightly soupy. Serve hot in individual soup or vegetable bowls or further prepare as Frijóles Refritos (see page 98).

Frijóles Refritos
(Refried Beans)
4 to 6 servings

In order to complete any Mexican feast, the "refries" must be mastered. They are served as a topping for tostadas, chalupas, or nachos and as a filling in chimis — the list continues endlessly.

The best "refries" unfortunately are cooked with lard — the more the better. Being health conscious as we are at Lista's, we choose to sacrifice some flavor for healthy cooking. We use only peanut oil or other pure vegetable oil for cooking at Lista's.

6 tablespoons cooking oil or lard
1 tablespoon chopped peeled onion
1 tablespoon minced peeled garlic
6 cups Frijóles de Olla (see page 97)
2 tablespoons flour

In a large heavy cast-iron skillet, heat oil or melt lard; add onion and garlic and sauté until tender. Add Frijóles de Olla (pinto beans), about 2 cups at a time, mashing with a potato masher and mixing with onion and garlic. Scrape off sides and bottom of skillet, blending into mixture. Continue to add beans and bean liquid as needed. Gradually stir in flour. Continue to cook over moderate heat, stirring frequently, until mixture is of desired consistency. Add bean liquid as necessary to achieve desired thickness.

Note: "Refries" freeze well, tightly covered, in freezer containers.

Gail's Favorite Fried Cabbage
6 servings

Fried cabbage was a specialty of my mother's as a quick-fix vegetable served with beans and chili, hot tortillas or Bunuelos (fried bread), and perhaps some Posole. One needs to originate from New Mexico or Colorado to imagine how wonderful those dishes taste together.

1 medium head (about 3 pounds) green cabbage
3 tablespoons cooking oil or butter or margarine
Salt and freshly ground pepper to taste

Remove the core from the cabbage and *very thinly* slice or shred remaining cabbage. Preheat a large heavy cast-iron or other heavy skillet over moderate heat; add oil or butter. When the oil is hot or the butter is melted, add cabbage. Stir-fry about 4 to 5 minutes, *until cabbage is tender but not limp. Be careful not to burn or scorch the cabbage.* Season to taste with salt and pepper. Serve immediately.

Mexicorn
6 to 8 servings

Although Mexicorn is an old recipe, we receive countless favorable comments about our corn side-dish. We serve this tasty vegetable with our Enchiladas de Pollo con Salsa Blanca.

1/2 cup chopped green bell pepper
1/2 cup chopped sweet red bell pepper
2 tablespoons minced peeled onion
1 teaspoon minced peeled garlic
2 tablespoons butter or margarine, melted
1 *fresh* jalapeño chile pepper, minced
6 cups whole-kernel corn (freshly cut from the cob, or
     thawed frozen, or drained canned)
1 teaspoon ground cumin

In a large heavy skillet, sauté bell peppers, onion, and garlic in butter over moderate heat until tender but not browned. Add jalapeño. Add corn and cumin, mixing well. Continue cooking for 2 to 3 minutes, stirring occasionally, until mixture is heated through. *Fresh* corn will require 2 to 3 additional minutes of cooking.

Papas de la Casa
(Potatoes of the House)
4 to 6 servings

2 pounds red-skinned potatoes, cut into 1-inch cubes (see note)
Salted boiling water as needed
2 tablespoons butter or *extra virgin* olive oil
1 small onion, peeled and cut into thin strips or coarsely chopped
1 small green bell pepper, cored, seeded, and cut into thin strips
     or coarsely chopped
1 jalapeño chile pepper, minced (optional)
1 teaspoon minced *fresh* or 1/2 teaspoon dried oregano
Pinch of ground cumin
Salt and freshly ground black pepper to taste
1 (6-ounce) can tomato juice

In a large heavy saucepan, cook potatoes, covered, in salted boiling water to cover until *just* tender, about 15 to 20 minutes; *do not overcook*. Drain well and set aside. In a large heavy cast-iron or other heavy skillet, melt butter or heat oil. Add onion and green bell pepper; sauté over moderate heat 2 to 3 minutes. Add potatoes, jalapeño, oregano, cumin, salt, and pepper; continue to sauté, stirring frequently, for 3 to 5 minutes. Reduce heat, add tomato juice, and simmer, covered, for about 5 minutes or until liquid is reduced by one half. Adjust seasoning as desired. Serve immediately as a side-dish for any entree.

Note: May use potatoes peeled or unpeeled, as desired.

Piñón Spinach
(Spinach with Pinenuts)
4 to 6 servings

4 cups cooked spinach (see note)
1/2 cup minced peeled onion
2 tablespoons hot *extra virgin* olive oil, or butter or margarine, melted
3/4 cup Lista's House Dressing (see index)
1/4 cup shelled piñóns (pinenuts) or Cantina Nuts (see index)

Cook spinach; drain well. In a medium heavy saucepan, sauté onion in olive oil over moderate heat for 1 to 2 minutes. Add spinach; bring mixture to a gentle simmer. Add dressing, tossing mixture lightly. Remove from heat and add pinenuts, tossing again to mix. Serve immediately.

Note: Cook stemmed whole fresh leaves in a small amount of boiling water for 1 to 2 minutes; drain well. Or, steam on a rack or in a steamer basket over 1/2 cup boiling water in a large heavy saucepan for 5 to 10 minutes or until tender but not soft or limp. The water should not touch the rack or basket.

Sautéed Southwestern-style Mixed Fresh Vegetables
4 to 6 servings

For many of our fajita specialties, we substitute a variety of sautéed fresh vegetables in place of the usual onions and bell peppers. These vegetables have become so popular that we have had to offer them as an alternative side-dish to the Mexican food staples of beans and rice. Everyone needs some variety!

1 cup sliced unpeeled zucchini squash
1 cup sliced unpeeled yellow (summer) squash
1 cup sliced peeled carrots
1 cup thinly sliced peeled red onion, separated into rings
1 cup thinly sliced sweet red bell pepper, cut into thin strips
1 cup sliced mushrooms
1/4 cup *extra virgin* olive oil
1 tablespoon soy sauce (optional) (see note)
1/2 teaspoon salt or to taste
1/2 teaspoon freshly ground black pepper or to taste
1/2 teaspoon granulated dried garlic or 1 garlic clove, peeled and minced
1/2 teaspoon New Mexico-style (bright red) chili powder

Prepare vegetables for sautéing. In a wok, heat oil to medium-high (375°F.) Add vegetables and stir-fry for 4 to 6 minutes until vegetables are *just* tender but not soft. Add seasonings, blending well. Serve immediately.

Note: May use sodium-reduced soy sauce, if desired.

Spanish Rice
4 to 6 servings

There are so many different ways to cook this staple of Mexican cuisine. Just about every Mexican household has its own recipe. As a side dish to serve with the main meal, I season my recipe mildly so that it does not overpower the entree.

2 tablespoons cooking oil
1 1/4 cups long-grain white rice
1 garlic clove, peeled and minced
1/2 cup chopped peeled onion
1/2 teaspoon white pepper or to taste
1/2 teaspoon ground cumin
1 teaspoon minced *fresh* or 1/2 teaspoon dried oregano
2 firm *ripe* large tomatoes, peeled and chopped
2 cups chicken stock or broth (see note)
1/2 cup *fresh* or frozen peas, thawed
Minced *fresh* cilantro for garnish

In a large heavy skillet, heat oil over moderate heat. Add rice; cook, stirring constantly, for 2 minutes. Add garlic and onion; continue to sauté for 1 minute. Stir in tomatoes and chicken stock; bring mixture to a boil. Reduce heat and simmer, covered, for 10 to 15 minutes. Add peas, if desired, and continue to cook, uncovered, for about 2 minutes. Garnish *each* serving with a sprinkle of cilantro.

Note: 1 1/2 (10 1/2-ounce) cans undiluted chicken broth may be substituted for homemade chicken stock or broth.

Cucumbers Southwest
6 to 8 servings

4 firm large cucumbers, peeled and thinly sliced
1 serrano chile pepper
1/2 cup *extra virgin* olive oil
1/2 cup red wine vinegar
1 tablespoon minced *fresh* or 1 1/2 teaspoons dried cilantro
1 tablespoon minced *fresh* or 1 1/2 teaspoons dried oregano
1 1/2 teaspoons freshly ground black pepper or to taste
1 teaspoon crushed dried hot red pepper or to taste
1/2 teaspoon minced peeled garlic

Prepare cucumbers. In a blender container, combine the remaining ingredients; cover and blend until mixture is liquified. Combine cucumbers and marinade in a deep medium bowl, coating cucumbers well. Cover and refrigerate for several hours to allow flavors to blend. To serve, drain and garnish as desired. Serve cold.

Dad's Potato Salad
8 to 10 servings

I try and try to prepare my dad's potato salad just as he made it. Sometimes it works. Like many recipes, just the right touch and practice are required for perfection. Cooking the potatoes to the correct doneness, so that the salad does not turn to mush or that the potatoes are not crunchy, is the secret to Dad's recipe.

2 1/2 pounds potatoes, cooked, drained, and cooled (see note)
5 hard-cooked eggs, peeled, cooled, and divided
1/2 (1-ounce) jar diced pimentos, drained (reserve 1 pimento
   strip for garnish)
1/4 cup chopped celery
2 tablespoons sweet pickle relish, drained
1 tablespoon chopped peeled onion
3/4 cup mayonnaise
1 tablespoon prepared mustard
1 tablespoon cider vinegar
Salt and freshly ground black pepper to taste

Peel potatoes and cut into bite-size pieces or cubes. Cut 3 eggs into thin slices or bite-size pieces. In a large bowl, combine potatoes, 3 cut-up eggs, pimento, celery, sweet pickle relish, and onion. Add mayonnaise, mustard, and vinegar, mixing gently, but well. Season with salt and pepper to taste; mix again. Cover and chill in the refrigerator. Cut remaining 2 hard-cooked eggs into wedges. Garnish potato salad with hard-cooked egg wedges and the reserved pimento strip. Serve cold.

Note: Potatoes may be peeled or unpeeled as desired. See page 99 for cooking directions. Potato salad will keep, covered, in the refrigerator for up to 4 days.

Ensalada de Pollo
(Chicken Salad)
4 to 5 servings

The taste of the main ingredient — chicken — should not be hidden — rather the other ingredients of the salad should complement its flavor.

1 pound boneless chicken breasts, skin removed, cooked, and cooled
1/2 cup chopped celery
2 tablespoons chopped peeled onion
1/2 cup mayonnaise
1 teaspoon celery salt
1 teaspoon minced *fresh* or 1/2 teaspoon dried cilantro
1 teaspoon freshly ground black pepper or to taste
1/8 teaspoon paprika
1/8 teaspoon curry powder (optional)

With a sharp knife, cut chicken into bite-size pieces or 1/2-inch cubes. In a large bowl, combine chicken, celery, and onion. Add mayonnaise and seasonings, mixing gently but well, being careful not to break-up chicken pieces. Cover and refrigerate for several hours to allow flavors to blend.

Taco Salad
one serving

Shredded iceberg lettuce as desired
1 crisp large flour tortilla shell
Coarsely crushed crisp corn chips as desired
1/3 cup shredded Monterey Jack cheese
1/3 cup chopped firm *ripe* tomato
1/2 cup (4 ounces) Pollo (chicken) or Meat Filling for Tacos,
    Enchiladas, or Burritos (see index)
1/4 cup Salsa Ranchera (see index)
3 tablespoons Lista's Guacamole (see index)

Spread about 1/3 cup shredded iceberg lettuce on a luncheon plate. Arrange tortilla shell over lettuce. Fill shell with lettuce and then corn chips as desired. Sprinkle cheese over chips on one side of the shell; sprinkle tomato over chips on opposite side of the shell. Top with meat of choice, then Salsa Ranchera. Garnish with Lista's Guacamole.

Variation: To prepare Marisco Salad, omit beef or chicken and guacamole. Add 4 ounces peeled deveined cooked shrimp or cooked scallops or cut-up cooked lobster or crabmeat.

Atún Blanca

(White Tuna Salad)

4 to 6 entree or 6 to 8 luncheon servings

2 pounds cooked *fresh* tuna or 5 (6 1/2-ounce) cans water-packed
   albacore tuna, drained (see note)
4 hard-cooked eggs, peeled and chopped
1/2 cup chopped celery
1/4 cup chopped peeled onion
1 1/2 cups mayonnaise
2 teaspoons white pepper or to taste
Salt to taste
Crisp leaf lettuce as desired for garnish
2 firm *ripe* medium tomatoes, cut into thin wedges

Cut cooked *fresh* tuna into bite-size pieces. Carefully flake canned tuna
with a fork into bite-size pieces. In a medium bowl, combine tuna, eggs,
celery, and onion. Add mayonnaise, pepper, and salt, mixing gently but
well. Arrange crisp leaf lettuce on chilled plates. Spoon tuna salad into the
center of *each* plate, dividing evenly. Garnish *each* with tomato wedges.

*Note: To cook fresh tuna, brush with 1 teaspoon melted butter or margarine or extra
virgin olive oil, then place in a hot skillet; quickly sauté, covered, over moderate to
high heat, about 2 minutes per side.*

Icy Hot Egg Salad

6 to 8 servings

*Serve chilled as a filling for sandwiches or as a snack, spread atop crisp crackers. I
also like to fill ripe tomatoes with this tasty mixture and serve as a refreshing
brunch item.*

10 hard cooked eggs, peeled and chilled
1/2 cup mayonnaise
1 teaspoon chopped chilpotle chile pepper in Adobo Sauce or dried chilpotle chile peppers
1 tablespoon minced pickled jalapeño chile peppers
1 tablespoon sweet pickle relish, undrained
1 teaspoon prepared mustard (see note)
1 teaspoon freshly ground black pepper
1/2 teaspoon paprika
2 to 4 drops Tabasco sauce
Salt to taste

Prepare eggs in advance and thoroughly chill in refrigerator. Finely chop
by hand. Or, place in a food process or blender container; cover and
process or blend until finely chopped. Combine all ingredients in a large
bowl, mixing gently. Cover and chill until ready to use. Salad mixture may
be stored, tightly covered, in the refrigerator for up to 48 hours.

Note: Preferably use bright yellow mustard usually served with hot dogs.

Hot Beef and Spinach Salad
4 servings

About every type of restaurant or other food service menu offers an entree salad or hot cooked seafood, poultry, or meat combined with crisp salad greens and other vegetables or fruits. Below is our offering.

4 hard-cooked eggs, peeled and cut into wedges
2 cups Lista's House Dressing (see index)
4 (6-ounce) beef skirt steaks, fat removed, cut into thick strips (see note)
1 tablespoon paprika
1 tablespoon ancho-style (dark) chili powder
1 tablespoon freshly ground black pepper
1 tablespoon jalapeño chili pepper powder
1 1/2 teaspoons salt or to taste
1 1/2 teaspoons garlic powder
1/2 teaspoon ground cumin
1/2 teaspoon ground dried oregano
2 pounds *fresh* spinach
2 firm *ripe* tomatoes, cut into thin wedges
2 cups thinly sliced mushrooms
1/4 cup shelled piñóns (pine nuts) or unsalted peanuts
Whole pitted black olives for garnish
1 *ripe* medium avocado, peeled, seed removed, cut into thin wedges and
    immediately sprinkled with lemon juice
Crisp tortilla chips warmed in a preheated very slow oven (250°F.)

Prepare eggs; cover and chill 30 minutes. Prepare Lista's House Dressing; set aside. In a large bowl, combine dry spices. Add meat strips, coating *each* lightly; set aside. Rinse spinach thoroughly in water, removing *all* grit and sand; dry between sheets of absorbent paper. Tear into bite-size pieces, removing stems. Divide spinach onto dinner plates.

Preheat a large heavy cast-iron or other heavy skillet over high heat until it starts to smoke. Shake off excess spice mixture from meat. Pan-fry beef strips quickly to medium rare or medium doneness, about 1 to 2 minutes per side. Divide onto salads, arranging attractively; sprinkle mushrooms and piñóns or peanuts over *each* salad. Garnish *each* with hard-cooked eggs, tomato, and avocado wedges. Accompany with warm tortilla chips. Pass Lista's House Dressing in a sauceboat.

Note: 1 1/2 pounds boneless beef sirloin, top round, or filet may be used.

Variation: 1 1/2 pounds boneless chicken breasts, cut into thin strips or 2 pounds medium (36 to 40 count) shrimp, peeled, deveined, and tails removed, may be used in place of the beef.

Southwestern Vinaigrette Dressing
about 2 3/4 cups

4 garlic cloves, peeled and chopped
1 cup red wine vinegar
1/2 cup chopped peeled onion
2 tablespoons minced *fresh* or 1 tablespoon dried cilantro
1 tablespoon crushed dried hot red pepper or to taste
2 teaspoons minced *fresh* or 1 teaspoon dried oregano
1 cup *extra virgin* olive oil or 1/2 cup olive oil and 1/2 cup other salad oil
Salt and freshly ground black pepper to taste

In a medium bowl, combine the first 6 ingredients, blending well. With a wire whisk, gradually add oil, whisking until mixture is smooth and well blended. Add salt and pepper to taste, whisking again to blend. Or, combine vinegar and oil in a blender container; cover and blend until mixture is smooth. Add remaining ingredients, stirring by hand to mix. Dressing may be stored in the refrigerator, tightly covered, in a glass container for up to 1 week.

Lista's House Dressing
about 4 1/2 cups

For several years, we've had many, many requests for our homemade salad dressing recipe. I would answer that someday it would be in a Lista's cookbook. Someday has finally arrived.

2 cups mayonnaise
1 cup milk
1/2 cup salad oil
1/2 cup grated Parmesan cheese
1/2 cup red wine vinegar
1 tablespoon lemon juice
1 tablespoon Worcestershire sauce
1 tablespoon Tabasco sauce or to taste
1 tablespoon freshly ground black pepper or to taste

In a deep medium bowl, combine all ingredients; beat well with a hand-rotary beater until smooth. Store in an airtight container in the refrigerator for up to 5 days. If dressing separates, rebeat with a hand-rotary beater or a wire whisk.

PANES
Y
POSTRES

Bolillos
(French rolls)
about 3 dozen rolls

3 cups boiling water
1/2 cup shortening, at room temperature
1/4 cup sugar
1 1/2 teaspoons salt
2 (1/4-ounce) packages (2 tablespoons) active dry yeast
About 8 cups flour, divided
Salt water (1 teaspoon salt dissolved in 1/4 cup water)

In a large bowl, combine boiling water, shortening, sugar, and salt, stirring until sugar and salt are dissolved; allow to cool to 105 to 115°F. Add yeast, beating well. Add 4 cups flour; mixing well. Cover and let rise in a warm place (85°F.) away from drafts until doubled in bulk, about 1 1/2 to 2 hours. Stir in enough of the remaining flour, 1/2 cup at a time, (about 3 cups), mixing well, to make a stiff dough.

Turn out onto a lightly floured surface; knead until smooth and elastic, about 5 minutes. Add flour as needed. Place dough in a greased large bowl, turning once to coat dough well. Cover and let rise again in a warm place (85°F.) until doubled in bulk, about 1 hour.

Turn dough out onto a lightly floured surface; knead gently two or three times. Divide dough into 20 equal-size pieces; shape *each* piece into a 3 x 2-inch rectangle. Arrange rolls on greased baking sheets, 2 inches apart. Cover and let rise again in a warm place (85°F.) until doubled in bulk, about 30 minutes. Brush *each* roll lightly with salt water *just* before baking. Bake in a preheated moderate oven (375°F.) until done and golden brown, about 20 minutes.

Churros
(Mexican Crullers)
about 20

Churros are a close relative to the batter cakes known as funnel cakes, a Pennsylvania Dutch specialty prepared by piping the batter through a funnel into hot oil. Most often these crullers are served with Mexican Hot Chocolate.

1 cup flour
1/2 teaspoon cinnamon
About 3 cups cooking oil for frying
1 cup water
5 tablespoons butter or margarine
1/8 teaspoon salt
3 eggs
Sifted confectioners' sugar as desired

Sift together the flour and cinnamon. Heat oil (1-inch in depth) in a large heavy skillet to medium-high (375°F.). In a medium heavy saucepan, bring water to a boil over high heat; add butter and salt, allowing butter to melt. Remove from heat. Add dry ingredients, mixing well with a wire whisk. Add eggs, one at a time, whisking well. Spoon into a pastry/piping bag fitted with a star-shaped tip. Squeeze batter in a straight line into hot oil, making *each* churro about 6 inches in length. Fry until crullers are golden brown, about 3 minutes, turning occasionally. Drain well on absorbent paper. Sift confectioners' sugar over churros. Serve warm.

Empanadas
(Little Pies)
about 8 to 10 turnovers

Popular at Christmastime in Mexico and the Southwest, Empanadas are pastry turn-overs filled with meat, fruit, or nuts. They can be served as an entree or in miniature form as hors d'oeuvres called Empanaditas.

2 cups sifted flour
2 teaspoons baking powder
1 teaspoon salt
2 tablespoons butter or margarine, at room temperature
Milk as needed
About 2 cups apricot or peach preserves
About 2 tablespoons apricot or peach brandy
About 4 to 5 cups cooking oil for deep-frying
Sifted confectioners' sugar as desired
Vanilla ice cream as desired (optional)

In a medium bowl, sift together the first 3 ingredients. With a pastry blender or 2 table knives, cut butter into dry ingredients, until mixture resembles coarse meal. Add about 3/4 cup milk, mixing well with a fork. Dough should be slightly sticky. Roll out dough on a lightly floured sur-face to a 1/8-inch thickness; cut dough into 2-inch circles with a 2-inch diameter biscuit cutter. Spoon a small amount of apricot or peach preser-ves onto *each* dough circle, slightly to one side of center; sprinkle *each* with 2 to 4 drops of brandy. Moisten edges of *each* and fold in half. Press edges together and flute with the tines of a fork.

Place Empanadas on ungreased baking sheets; bake in a preheated hot oven (425°F.) fro 12 to 15 minutes or until pastry is done and lightly browned. Empanadas may be prepared in advance, placed on baking sheets, tightly covered, and stored in the refrigerator for 2 to 3 days or in the freezer for up to 6 months. Allow 3 to 4 minutes extra baking time if refrigerated and 5 to 7 minutes if frozen.

Variation: Use Pollo or Meat Filling for Tacos, Enchiladas, or Burritos (see index) in place of fruit preserves.

Tortilla

The tortilla is the traditional bread served in New Mexico. It is prepared with harina (flour) or maze (corn). Usually tortillas are the only Mexican-style breads found in restaurants of New Mexico; however, if you are fortunate enough to find a panadería (bakery), you will soon learn of the numerous panes (breads) available. There are many colorful and creative breads and cookies available with imaginative names, collectively known as pan dulce (sweet breads).

Jalapeño Corn Bread
8 servings

1 cup sifted flour
3 teaspoons sugar
3 teaspoons baking powder
1 teaspoon salt
1/2 teaspoon baking soda
1 1/2 cups yellow cornmeal
3 eggs, beaten
1 cup milk
1/4 cup cooking oil
1 (8-ounce) can whole-kernel corn, drained
1 jalapeño chile pepper, seeded and minced
1/4 cup minced sweet red bell pepper

In a medium bowl, sift together the first 5 ingredients. Add cornmeal, mixing well. In a 2-cup measure, combine eggs, milk, and oil, mixing well with a wire whisk or fork; add all at once to the dry ingredients, mixing *just* until dry ingredients are well moistened. Stir in corn, jalapeño, and sweet red pepper. Spoon into a lightly greased 9-inch round layer pan or an 8 x 8 x 2-inch baking pan, spreading evenly. Bake in a preheated moderate oven (375°F.) for 25 to 30 minutes or until done and lightly browned. Cut into wedges or squares and serve hot or at room temperature.

Variation: To prepare muffins, spoon prepared batter into greased muffin pans, 2 3/4 inches in diameter, dividing evenly. Bake as previously directed for 20 to 25 minutes or until done.

Gorditas
(Stuffed Tortillas)
about 12 to 15 pieces

Gorditas are stuffed corn tortillas usually served around brunch time. Pianda, a small restaurant in Monterey, Mexico serves many varieties of these little treasures. With many eateries in Monterey and Guadalahara, one can watch the wonderful art of tortilla, Gordita, and Sopaipilla making at the cocina al arie libre (open-air kitchens). Visitors can also purchase some of these goodies to take home if they can keep from entering the eatery and gorging on the specialties. I wonder if that's where the word gordita really originates?

2 pounds corn masa (see note)
8 ounces lean ground beef
1 garlic clove, peeled and minced
1/2 cup minced peeled onion
2 medium potatoes, cooked, peeled, and cut into 1/2-inch cubes (see note)
1 jalapeño chile pepper, minced
1 cup shredded Monterey Jack cheese (optional)
1 tablespoon minced *fresh* or 1 1/2 teaspoons dried cilantro
1 1/2 teaspoons salt
About 2 to 3 cups cooking oil for frying Gorditas

Prepare masa dough as in preparation for regular tortillas; cover and set aside. In a medium heavy skillet, thoroughly brown ground beef over moderate heat, stirring occasionally and breaking up any clumps of meat; drain off excess drippings. Add garlic and onion and continue cooking, stirring frequently, until the onion is *just* tender. Add potatoes, jalapeño, cilantro, and salt, mixing well; mash slightly to make the stuffing slightly sticky so it will hold together. Set stuffing aside.

Separate prepared masa dough into 3-ounce balls. Roll out *each* ball into a 6-inch diameter circle. Spoon about 1/2 cup (2 ounces) stuffing mixture onto the middle of *each*. Shape the dough around the stuffing, taking care there are no holes in the dough to allow stuffing to seep out. Shape *each* filled dough "package" into a square similar to ravioli, *little pillows*.

In a large heavy skillet, heat oil to medium (350°F.). Add Gorditas and pan-fry, turning occasionally, until they are crisp and golden brown, about 3 to 4 minutes. Drain well on absorbent paper. Serve hot.

Note: Corn masa is available in many specialty food stores.

Note: Cook potatoes in boiling salted water to cover for about 15 minutes. Do not overcook.

Sopaipillas
(Crispy Puffed Bread With Cinnamon Sugar Coating)
about 20

Of Mexican and Indian origin, Sopaipillas are presented as the very first course in many New Mexican restaurants that feature traditional Spanish or Mexican food. When the small pieces of dough are cooked in hot oil, they puff out and form bread with a crispy crust and hollow center. They are served hot, coated with honey, or rolled in cinnamon sugar.

2 cups sifted flour
2 teaspoons baking powder
1 teaspoon sugar (optional)
1/4 teaspoon salt
1 tablespoon shortening, at room temperature
3/4 cup lukewarm water (80 to 90°F.)
About 1 1/2 cups cooking oil for deep-frying
Cinnamon sugar for garnishing (optional)
Honey for dipping (optional)

In a medium bowl, sift together the flour, baking powder, sugar, if desired, and salt. With a pastry blender or 2 table knives or the hands, cut in shortening until mixture resembles cornmeal. Add water, mixing well with a fork. Turn dough out onto a lightly floured surface; knead until dough is smooth. Cover and allow to stand for 20 minutes. Cut dough into 4 equal pieces. Roll out *each* dough piece to a 1/8-inch thickness. Cut rolled dough into equal-size small triangles.

In a deep-fryer or medium heavy saucepan, heat oil (3 to 4-inch depth) to hot (400°F.). Carefully drop dough triangles, one at a time, into hot oil. Deep-fry, turning *each* constantly, for about 30 seconds or until dough triangles are puffed and golden brown. Drain on absorbent paper. Serve warm. Or, sprinkle *each* lightly with cinnamon sugar and serve as a sweet. May serve with honey for dipping, if desired.

Aunt Phyllis' Bischochitos
(Mexican Holiday Cookies)
6 to 7 dozen

These cookies, made with a hint of anise flavoring, are a Christmas tradition made by many New Mexico families. The name comes from the Mexican Indian word for biscuit or cake. Although my family has used lard in the cookies over the years, shortening is a more healthy choice.

6 cups sifted flour
3 teaspoons baking powder
1 teaspoon salt
2 cups shortening

1 cup sugar
2 eggs, at room temperature
1 tablespoon Anisette or Sambuca liqueur
1/4 cup sweet dessert wine or sweet vermouth
1 tablespoon anise seeds (optional)

Sift together the first 3 ingredients; set aside. In a large bowl, cream shortening thoroughly. Gradually add sugar, beating until light and fluffy. Add
eggs, one at a time, and liqueur, beating well. Stir in dry ingredients, wine,
and anise seeds, if desired, mixing well to form a soft dough.

Shape dough into a flat patty. Roll out half the dough at a time on a lightly
floured board to a 1/4-inch thickness. Cut into fancy shapes or 2-inch
rounds with lightly floured cookie cutters.

Arrange cookies on very lightly-greased baking sheets. Bake in a preheated
moderate oven (350°F.) for 12 to 15 minutes, or until done. Cookies do not
brown but remain cream-colored. Cool on wire racks.

Flan de Caramelo
(Caramel Custard)
10 to 12 servings

Flan de Caramelo is the classic dessert of Mexico—smooth and oh so satisfying.

1/4 cup plus 2 tablespoons sugar, divided
1 1/2 cups evaporated milk
3/4 cup heavy cream
4 eggs
3 egg yolks
1/4 teaspoon nutmeg
1/4 teaspoon cinnamon
Sweetened flavored whipped cream for garnish (optional)

Evenly spread 1/4 cup sugar in one layer over the bottom of an 8-inch
round layer pan. Place pan over low to moderate heat, stirring sugar constantly, until it turns a dark caramel color. Allow to cool.

In a medium bowl, combine evaporated milk, cream, eggs, egg yolks, 2
tablespoons sugar, nutmeg, and cinnamon. Beat at high speed of an
electric mixer for 10 to 15 seconds. Pour mixture into prepared round layer
pan over caramelized sugar. Place custard-filled pan in a larger pan filled
with about 1/2 to 3/4 inch of hot water.

Bake in a preheated slow oven (325°F.) for 45 minutes or until a table knife
inserted in the center of the custard comes out clean. Cool and then chill
for at least 6 hours.

To serve, invert custard onto a chilled serving plate; tap the pan lightly
and shake gently to release the custard onto the plate. Garnish Flan with
sweetened flavored whipped cream, if desired.

Helados Fritas
(Fried Ice Cream)
6 servings

Yes — the ice cream is deep-fried! The trick to keeping it from melting is to deep-fry for only a few seconds. This dessert has acquired rave reviews accompanied with many oohs and aahs. You can receive the same response if you're willing to do the work required. Even though I'm divulging my secret, I'm confident you will much rather be served this dessert at Lista's.

2 quarts vanilla-flavored ice cream, slightly softened
2 cups cornflakes
1 cup unsalted peanuts
2 eggs, at room temperature
1/2 cup honey
About 3 to 4 cups canola or peanut oil for deep-frying
Chocolate syrup or hot fudge sauce and/or sweetened flavored whipped
   cream for garnish

Form softened ice cream into 6 equal-size balls; freeze until balls are very hard. Combine cornflakes and peanuts together in a food processor or blender container; cover and process or blend until mixture is finely ground. Transfer mixture to a deep medium bowl. In a deep small bowl, combine eggs and honey, beating lightly with a wire whisk.

When ice cream balls are frozen *very hard*, remove one at a time from freezer and dip into egg mixture and then into cornflake-peanut mixture, coating well. Place on an ungreased baking sheet and return to the freezer for at least 1 hour or longer. Repeat process for *each* ice cream ball.

Heat oil (about 5 inches in depth) to medium-low (325°F.) in a large heavy saucepan or deep-fryer. Have all garnishes ready before starting to deep-fry frozen ice cream balls. Using a slotted spoon, lower one ice cream ball at a time into the hot oil for 10 to 15 seconds, (A small amount of coating will come off of *each* ball during the deep-frying process.) Shake off excess oil or quickly drain on absorbent paper. Place *each* on a dessert plate, garnish with chocolate syrup or hot fudge sauce, and/or sweetened flavored whipped cream.

Mexican Wine Cookies
about 4 dozen

4 cups sifted flour
1/2 teaspoon salt
1 cup butter or margarine, at room temperature
1 cup sugar
1 egg, at room temperature

1/4 cup cream sherry
Sifted confectioners' sugar, as needed

Sift flour and salt together; set aside. In a large bowl, cream butter thoroughly. Gradually add sugar, beating until light and fluffy. Add egg, beating well. Gradually stir in sherry, mixing until sherry is blended into dough. Shape mixture into 3/4-inch balls or 1 1/2 x 1/2-inch oval cakes.

Arrange cookies on ungreased baking sheets, 2 inches apart; bake in a preheated moderate oven (375°F.) for 10 to 12 minutes or until done and lightly browned. Remove cookies from oven and allow to cool for 1 minute on baking sheets. On a sheet of wax paper, roll warm cookies in confectioners' sugar, coating *each* well. Store at room temperature in an air-tight container.

Margarita Cheesecake
12 servings

16 graham crackers, finely crushed
3 (8-ounce) packages cream cheese, at room temperature
4 eggs, at room temperature
3 cups sour cream, divided
1 cup plus 1 tablespoon sugar, divided
3 tablespoons *fresh* lime juice
3 to 4 tablespoons Jose Cuervo or 1800 Gold tequila
1 tablespoon *fresh* lemon juice
1 to 2 tablespoons Triple Sec liqueur or to taste
6 to 8 drops green food coloring (optional)

Spread graham cracker crumbs in one even layer over the bottom of a 9-inch round spring-form pan; set aside.

In a large bowl, beat cream cheese until smooth. Add eggs, one at a time, 2 cups sour cream, 1 cup sugar, lime juice, tequila, lemon juice, and Triple Sec, beating well. Spoon filling over graham cracker crumbs in pan. Bake in a preheated moderate oven (350°F.) for 50 to 60 minutes. (If cheesecake begins to brown too much, cover with aluminum foil and reduce oven temperature to slow (325°F.). Cool thoroughly. With a table knife, loosen the sides of the cheesecake from pan; release spring-form and place cheesecake on a serving plate.

In a small bowl, combine remaining 1 cup sour cream, 1 tablespoon sugar, and green food coloring, if desired, mixing well. Evenly spoon over cake; refrigerate until ready to serve. Cut into wedges as desired.

Peras al Vino
(Pears in Wine)
12 servings

12 firm *ripe* Bartlett pears, peeled, stems intact
8 cups water
4 cups red sangria or sweet red wine
2 1/4 cups piloncillo (see note) or dark brown sugar, firmly packed
1/4 cup Amaretto liqueur
2 cinnamon sticks, *each* broken in half
Sweetened flavored whipped cream or vanilla ice cream for
    garnish (optional)

Prepare pears for cooking. In a medium roasting pan or Dutch oven, combine water, sangria, brown sugar, Amaretto, and cinnamon sticks; bring to a boil over high heat and continue to boil for 25 to 30 minutes, until the amount of syrup is reduced by one half. Add pears, basting *each* well with the syrup; reduce heat to moderate and poach pears for 15 to 20 minutes or until fork tender, turning pears frequently. *Do not overcook, or allow pears to become mushy.* Remove from heat and transfer to the refrigerator until pears and syrup are thoroughly chilled. Serve chilled or at room temperature in dessert bowls. Spoon syrup over *each* serving and garnish with sweetened flavored whipped cream or vanilla ice cream.

Note: A coarse dark, less refined Mexican brown sugar available in many Mexican specialty food markets. It has a flavor which is a cross between brown sugar and molasses.

Kahlúa Mousse
6 to 8 servings

2/3 cup sugar, divided
2 tablespoons cocoa
2 tablespoons instant coffee crystals
1/2 cup Kahlúa liqueur
5 large eggs, at room temperature and separated
2 cups heavy cream, chilled

In a small heavy saucepan, combine 1/3 cup sugar, cocoa, and coffee crystals; add Kahlúa, blending well. Stir over low heat until sugar is dissolved. *Do not boil.* In a small bowl, lightly beat egg yolks with a fork, then add to Kahlúa mixture, blending well. Cook over low heat, stirring constantly, for 1 minute. Remove from heat and refrigerate until mixture is cool. In a large bowl, beat egg whites until frothy; gradually add remaining sugar, beating until stiff, glossy, but not dry, peaks are formed. Gently fold Kahlúa mixture into egg whites, being careful not to overmix. In a chilled medium bowl, beat the cream with chilled beaters, until stiff peaks are formed; reserve a small amount for garnish. Fold whipped cream into beaten egg white mixture, folding *just* until mousse is an even, light tan color. Spoon into 6 to 8 sherbet or wine glasses. Chill in refrigerator for at least 1 hour before serving.

Santa Fe Bread Pudding with Lemon Tequila Sauce

8 to 10 servings

Old-fashioned bread pudding acquires a unique flavor in our offering. Hmm good!

8 ounces French bread, torn into bite-size pieces
1 (8-ounce) can crushed pineapple, including juice
3 eggs, at room temperature and beaten
2 cups milk
3/4 cup light brown sugar, firmly packed
1/2 cup dark seedless raisins
1/4 cup chopped pecans or English walnuts
1/4 teaspoon cinnamon
Lemon Tequila Sauce (see index)

Arrange bread pieces in one layer on an ungreased baking sheet; bake in a preheated slow oven (325°F.) for 8 to 10 minutes or until bread pieces are lightly browned. In a large bowl, combine the remaining ingredients, mixing well. Fold in toasted bread pieces; allow mixture to stand until all the liquid is absorbed, about 15 to 20 minutes. Spoon mixture into a greased 13 x 9 x 2-inch baking dish. Bake, covered, in a preheated moderate oven (350°F.) for 45 minutes or until a table knife inserted in the center comes out clean. Allow to cool to warm. To serve, cut into squares. Liberally spoon hot Lemon Tequila Sauce over *each* serving.

Luscious Lemon Meringue Pie
one 9-inch pie

Unbaked pie shell (9-inch) (see note)
1 cup sugar
1/2 cup corn starch
1/4 teaspoon salt
2 cups boiling water
5 egg yolks, at room temperature and lightly beaten
1/3 cup *fresh* lemon juice
2 tablespoons butter or margarine, at room temperature
Basic Meringue

Prick unbaked pie shell all over with the tines of a fork. Bake prepared pie shell in a preheated hot oven (425°F.) for 10 to 12 minutes or until golden brown. Remove and cool on a wire rack.

In a 2-quart heavy saucepan, combine sugar, corn starch, and salt. Gradually add boiling water, blending until mixture is dissolved. Cook, stirring constantly, over moderate heat, until mixture starts to thicken; remove from heat. In a small bowl, combine egg yolks and lemon juice; stir mixture into hot filling. Return filling to a low heat; continue to cook, stirring constantly, for 2 minutes. Add butter, blending well. Spoon filling into cooled pie shell.

Prepare meringue and carefully spread over filling, sealing meringue to the edges of the crust. Bake in a preheated moderate oven (350°F.) for 12 to 15 minutes or until meringue is lightly browned. Cool pie on a wire rack away from drafts before serving.

Note: Use favorite one-crust pie recipe or one half pastry recipe from Kathy's Apple Pie (see index)

Basic Meringue

5 egg whites, at room temperature
1/4 teaspoon cream of tartar
1/4 cup sugar
1/2 teaspoon lemon juice

In a large bowl, combine the egg whites and cream of tartar; beat until egg whites are foamy. Gradually add sugar, beating until soft glossy peaks are formed. Sprinkle lemon juice over egg whites and continue beating for an additional few seconds. Proceed as directed above in pie recipe.

Kathy's Apple Pie
one 9-inch pie

Crust
2 cups sifted flour
2 teaspoons salt
3/4 cup shortening
1/4 to 1/3 cup warm water

Filling
6 (about 2 pounds) tart cooking apples (see note)
3/4 cup light brown sugar, firmly packed
1/2 cup sugar
1/3 cup butter or margarine, at room temperature
1/4 cup molasses or maple syrup
2 teaspoons cinnamon or to taste
1 1/2 teaspoons apple pie spice or 1 teaspoon nutmeg
   and 1/2 teaspoon ground cloves
3/4 teaspoon salt
1/4 cup heavy or sour cream
1 tablespoon lemon juice

In a medium bowl, sift together flour and salt; cut shortening into flour with a pastry blender or 2 table knives, until the mixture is the texture of coarse meal. Or, work flour and shortening together with the hands. *Do not overmix.* Sprinkle water evenly over surface, mixing lightly with a fork until particles hold together and leave the sides of the bowl. Shape into a ball, kneading lightly; divide dough into two equal-size balls. Cover and allow to stand at room temperature while preparing filling.

Peel apples, leaving some of the peel intact; with a sharp knife, thinly slice, discarding core and seeds. In a large bowl, combine brown sugar, sugar, butter, molasses or maple syrup, and spices, beating until smooth and sugar is dissolved. Add apples, mixing lightly. Add heavy or sour cream and lemon juice, mixing again. Adjust seasoning.

On a lightly floured board, roll out half of the dough into a circle 1/8-inch thick and 1 1/4 inches larger in diameter than inverted pie plate. Carefully fit crust into pie plate. Trim crust edge, leaving a 1/2-inch overhang. Spoon apple filling into pie shell.

Roll out remaining dough into a circle 1/8-inch thick and 1 inch larger in diameter than top of inverted pie plate. Cut small designs or slits in center of top crust for steam vents. Moisten edges of lower crust. Cover with top crust and press edges of two crusts together. Trim crust 1/2 inch beyond edge of pie plate and press edges together to seal. Fold edges under bottom crust and flute with the fingers or tines of a fork.

Cover edges of the crust with strips of aluminum foil. Bake in a preheated moderate oven (375°F.) for 40 minutes. Remove foil, reduce oven temperature to slow (325°F.) and continue baking for 15 minutes. Allow pie to cool for at least 30 minutes before serving.

Note: Use a tart variety apple such as Winesap, Granny Smith, or McIntosh.

Mangos con Salsa de Plantano y Fresca
(Mangos with Plantain Strawberry Sauce)
6 servings

6 firm *ripe* mangos, peeled
1 pound plantains or firm *ripe* bananas, peeled and sliced
2 cups *ripe* strawberries, hulled
1 cup sugar
1/2 cup Kahlúa liqueur
24 firm *ripe* strawberries for garnish (12 remaining whole and 12 sliced)
24 sprigs of mint for garnish

With a sharp knife, cut mangos in half; cover and refrigerate until mangos are thoroughly chilled. In a blender or food processor container, combine plantains or bananas, 2 cups hulled strawberries, sugar, and Kahlúa; cover and blend or process until mixture is a purée. Arrange a mango slice on *each* of six oversized dessert plates; liberally spoon fruit purée over *each* mango. Garnish *each* with whole and sliced strawberries and a sprig of mint.

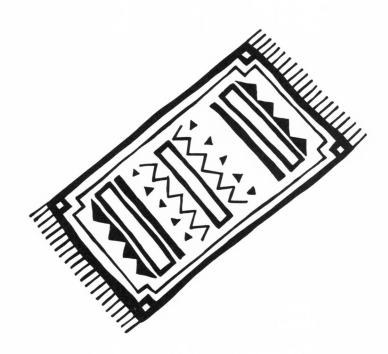

BEBIDAS

Agua de Sandía
(Watermelon Frappe)
12 to 14 servings

4 1/2 pounds red or yellow-fleshed watermelon
8 cups cold water
3 cups sugar
2 tablespoons grenadine
Pinch of salt
8 cups ice cubes
Sprigs of *fresh* **mint for garnish**

With a sharp knife, remove the rind from the watermelon and discard. Cut the remaining melon meat into small chunks; remove seeds and discard. Combine some of the melon, water, and sugar in a blender container; cover and blend at high speed until mixture is a thick purée. Pour purée into a 1 1/2 to 2-gallon container. Repeat process until all but 3 cups of melon are puréed; reserve 3 cups melon chunks. Add grenadine and salt to purée, blending well. Add reserved melon and ice cubes, blending well by hand. Serve immediately in tall (iced tea) glasses. Garnish *each* with a sprig of mint.

Americans didn't start migrating from the East toward New Mexico until 1821 when the Santa Fe trail was established. This route was one of the earliest links between the East and the American Southwest. New Mexico is also home to the country's oldest road, El Camino Real.

Agua Fresca de Limon Verde
(Fresh Lime Beverage)
8 servings

In the central markets of Mexico and New Mexico, refreshing fresh fruit beverages are very popular. Women grind lime peels in Molcajetes (mortars and pestles) to extract the green oils which color the limeade.

8 cups cold water
1 1/2 cups sugar
1 1/2 cups *fresh* **lime juice**
1/2 cup *fresh*ly **grated lime peel**
3 cups ice cubes
Additional ice cubes for glasses
Thin lime slices or wedges for garnish

Combine water and sugar in a 1-gallon container, stirring to dissolve sugar. Add lime juice, lime peel, and ice cubes. Place desired amount of ice cubes in *each* of 8 tall iced tea glasses. Pour limeade over ice in glasses; garnish *each* with a thin lime slice or wedge.

Bloody María
(Bloody Mary)
12 servings

Nothing goes better with a Sunday brunch of Huevos Rancheros or Machaca with warm tortillas than an ice cold Bloody María —- a zesty version of the Bloody Mary.

Salt as desired
1 to 2 limes, cut into thin wedges
1 (46-ounce) can tomato juice, divided
1 cup Jose Cuervo or 1800 Gold tequila, divided
1/4 cup *fresh* lime juice, divided
2 tablespoons Worcestershire sauce
2 tablespoons minced *fresh* cilantro, divided
Ice cubes as desired for garnish
Additional limes as desired for garnish, cut into thin wedges

Spread a layer of salt in a saucer. Rub a lime wedge around the outside rim of *each* of 12 tall (iced tea) glasses, then roll *each* glass rim in salt, coating *each* well. In a blender container, combine half of the tomato juice, half of the tequila, 2 tablespoons lime juice, 1 tablespoon Worcestershire sauce, and 1 tablespoon cilantro. Season with salt as desired. Pour mixture into a large pitcher. Repeat process for remaining ingredients. Place ice cubes as desired in *each* glass. Pour tomato-tequila mixture over ice cubes. Garnish *each* with a thin lime wedge. Serve immediately.

Café de Olla
(Clay Pot Coffee)
6 to 7 servings

4 ounces piloncillo or 1/2 cup light brown sugar, firmly packed
2 cinnamon sticks
2 whole cloves
8 cups cold water
1/2 cup freshly ground coffee beans of choice
Additional cinnamon sticks for garnish.

In a large heavy saucepan, combine piloncillo, cinnamon, and cloves; bring to a boil over high heat. Reduce temperature, cover, and simmer for 5 minutes. Stir in coffee, increase heat, and return to a boil. Strain and serve immediately. Garnish *each* serving with a cinnamon stick as a stirrer.

Champaña Pera
(Pear Champagne)
one serving

About 1 ounce (2 tablespoons) pear nectar (see note)
Sugar as desired
Dash of Angostura bitters
About 3 ounces (1/3 cup) champagne, chilled

Dip the rim of a chilled champagne glass in the pear nectar and then coat in sugar as desired. Add remaining pear nectar and bitters to the champagne glass. Garnish as desired. Serve immediately.

Note: Available in the canned fruit juice section of most grocery stores.

Café Mexicano
(Mexican Coffee)
one serving

1 ounce (2 tablespoons) Kahlúa liqueur
1/2 ounce (1 tablespoon) brandy
1 teaspoon chocolate syrup
About 3/4 to 1 cup hot prepared strong-brewed coffee
Sweetened flavored whipped cream for garnish
Grated bittersweet or semi-sweet chocolate for garnish

Combine Kahlúa, brandy, and chocolate syrup in a coffee mug, blending well. Fill mug with coffee, blending slightly. Top with sweetened flavored whipped cream and a sprinkle of grated chocolate.

Mango Daiquiri
8 servings

12 large *fresh* mangos, peeled, seeds removed, and thinly sliced, divided
2 (16-ounce) cans sliced peeled mangos, divided
16 cups ice cubes, divided
2 cups (16-ounces) dark rum, divided
Sugar to taste

In a blender container, combine 4 *fresh* mangos and half of a 16-ounce can of mangos; cover and blend at high speed until mixture is puréed. Add ice as desired and 1/2 cup rum; cover and blend again until mixture is a frappe and ice is well crushed. Pour mixture into a large pitcher. Repeat process three times. Pour frappe into cocktail glasses, garnish as desired, and serve immediately.

Classic Margarita
one serving

1 lime wedge for coating glass
Salt as desired
2 ounces (1/4 cup) tequila
2 tablespoons *fresh* lime juice
3/4 ounce (1 1/2 tablespoons) Triple Sec liqueur
1 tablespoon *fresh* lemon juice
Ice cubes as desired
Additional lime wedge for garnish

Rub the cut surface of a lime wedge around the rim of a stemmed Margarita or short cocktail glass. Immediately dip the glass edge in salt, coating well; set aside. Combine the remaining ingredients, except ice, in a cocktail shaker; cover and shake vigorously. Strain mixture into the prepared stemmed Margarita glass. Or, do not strain, add ice cubes to the prepared short cocktail glass, and pour tequila mixture over the ice. Garnish with a lime wedge.

Worms of wisdom!!!

Many of us think of tequila as a strong potable, but tequila is to Mexico what Cognac is to France: a regulated liquor produced only in a specific region. Mezcal, tequila's country cousin, is more robust and rustic. That's the powerful libation that has the worm in it — a tradition that's supposed to indicate the ripeness of the agave plant from which it was distilled. Gold tequila refers to the tequila being aged in oak.

Rompope
(Rum Eggnog)
4 servings

3 cups milk
1 1/4 cups sugar
6 egg yolks, at room temperature
1/4 teaspoon vanilla extract
6 ounces (3/4 cup) dark rum
Freshly grated nutmeg for garnish

In a large heavy saucepan, combine milk and sugar; stir over moderate heat until mixture is reduced slightly in volume. Cool. In a large bowl, beat egg yolks until they are thick and light yellow in color. Add egg yolks to milk, beating well with a wire whisk or hand-rotary or electric beater. Add vanilla. Return to heat, reduce temperature, and cook *just* until mixture begins to simmer. *Do not boil.* Cool 10 minutes. Gradually add rum, beating well. Pour into a glass container, cover, and chill thoroughly. To serve, pour eggnog into punch cups and garnish *each* with freshly grated nutmeg.

Sangrita de Tomate
(Spicy Tomato Beverage)
4 servings

4 *ripe* small tomatoes, peeled and seeded
2 1/2 cups tomato juice
Serrano chile peppers, seeded, as desired, divided
1 cup orange juice
1 tablespoon chopped peeled onion
1 tablespoon *fresh* lime juice
2 teaspoons sugar
Salt as desired
4 lime slices or wedges

In a blender container, combine tomatoes, tomato juice, 1 chile pepper, orange juice, onion, lime juice, sugar, and 1/4 teaspoon salt; cover and blend at high speed for 30 seconds. Add additional salt and serrano chile peppers to taste; cover and blend again until smooth. Chill thoroughly. Serve over ice, if desired, in tall (iced tea) glasses. Garnish *each* serving with a slice or wedge of lime.

Variation: Add 2 ounces (1/4 cup) vodka and ice cubes to each salt-coated tall glass. Fill each with tomato mixture and garnish with a slice or wedge of lime.

Tamarindo
(Mango and Tamarind Beverage)
one serving

Tamarind paste may be found in most Middle East or Southeast Asian grocery stores. The paste is prepared from the tropical Tamarind fruit. This beverage was created to accompany hot spicy foods.

1/4 cup mango juice
1 ounce (2 tablespoons) dark or lemon-flavored rum
2 tablespoons *fresh* orange juice
1 tablespoon tamarind paste
Ice cubes as desired
A thin mango slice for garnish

In a blender container, combine the first 4 ingredients; add ice as desired. Cover and blend at high speed until mixture is smooth and ice is well crushed. Pour mixture into a stemmed cocktail, martini, or wine glass and garnish with a slice of mango. Serve immediately.

Gold Margarita
one serving

1 lime wedge
Salt as desired
2 ounces (1/4 cup) Jose Cuervo Gold or 1800 tequila
2 tablespoons *fresh* lime juice
3/4 ounce (1 1/2 tablespoons) Grand Mariner liqueur
1 tablespoon *fresh* lemon juice
Ice cubes as desired

To prepare a Gold Margarita, follow the directions for preparing a Classic Margarita (see index). Many people like to float the Grand Mariner liqueur on top of the cocktail instead of shaken with the other ingredients.

Mexican Hot Chocolate
4 servings

3 squares (ounces) semi-sweet chocolate, grated
4 cups milk
1/4 cup sugar
1/2 teaspoon vanilla extract
1/4 teaspoon cinnamon
4 cinnamon sticks

In a medium heavy saucepan, combine all ingredients; bring to a boil over moderate heat. Beat mixture with a hand-rotary beater. Allow mixture to return to a boil. Beat again until mixture becomes very frothy. Serve imme-diately in chocolate cups or mugs. Garnish *each* with a stick of cinnamon.

Tequila del Sol
(Tequila Sunrise)
one serving

Ice cubes as desired
5 ounces (5/8 cup) orange juice (see note)
1 1/2 ounces (3 tablespoons) tequila
2 teaspoons *fresh* lime juice
2 teaspoons grenadine
A thin half slice of orange and a sprig of *fresh* mint for garnish

In a 12-ounce cocktail glass, fill with ice cubes as desired, add orange juice, tequila, and lime juice, mixing slightly. Add grenadine, slowly pouring into the glass at one edge (the grenadine will settle to the bottom of the glass). Garnish with a half slice of orange and a mint sprig.

Note: Use freshly squeezed orange juice for best flavor.

Sangria de la Casa
(Wine Punch of the House)
8-10 servings

Every Mexican fiesta deserves at least one pitcher of refreshing fruity Sangria. This is a recipe for which I'm sure you'll find many excuses to prepare.

1 (750-milliter) bottle dry red (table) wine
2 (16-ounce) cans apple juice
1 (16-ounce) can carbonated (7-up) beverage
1 (6-ounce) can pineapple juice
1 (6-ounce) can cranberry juice
2 ounces (1/4 cup) cherry-flavored brandy
2 ounces (1/4 cup) apricot-flavored brandy
Ice cubes as desired
2 large apples, cored, seeded, and cut into small cubes or pieces
2 seedless oranges, peeled and cut into small pieces

Combine the first 7 ingredients together in a large glass pitcher, stirring vigoursly. Add ice as desired and apple and orange pieces. Serve in tall (iced tea) glasses, adding some of the ice and fruit to *each* serving.

MENÚS

Cocktail Get-Together with a Southwestern Flair

Cantina Nuts
page 15

Quesadillas
page 22

Taquitos
page 23

Southwestern Bean Dip
page 17

Lista's Guacamole
pages 18-19

Crisp Tortilla Chips

Barbecued Chicken Tacos
page 37

Classic Margaritas
page 125

Mango Daiquiris
page 124

Chilled Soft Drinks

Chilled Dry White Wine

Chilled Cervecas

Iced Tea

South by Southwest Picnic or Picnic Olé

P B & J's
page 21

Gazpacho
page 29

Burgers Galore   Cilantro Chicken
page 40   pages 48-49

Dad's Potato Salad   Cucumbers Southwestern-Style
page 102   page 102

Jalapeño Corn Bread
page 110

Peach Salsa
page 87

Seasonal Fresh Fruit

Kathy's Apple Pie   Mexican Wine Cookies
page 119   pages 114-115

Agua Fresca de Limon Verde   Chilled Cervecas
page 122

Chilled Dry White Wine

Week-end Brunch le Ruben

Tequila de Sol
page 127

Bloody Mariás
page 123

Corn Salsa
page 83

Crisp Tortilla Chips

Huevos Rancheros con Salsa Roja
page 62

Beef Enchiladas New Mexico-Style
page 38

Machaca
page 62

Grilled Chorizo Patties
page 48

Papas de la Casa
page 99

Frijóles Refritos
page 98

Guacamole Salad

Churros
pages 108-109

Sopaipillas
pages 112-113

Kalhúa Mousse
page 116

Café de Olla
page 123

Dinner In The Lista's Manner

Sangria de la Casa
page 128

Ceviche de Mariscos
page 16

Chimayo Corn Chowder
pages 28-29

Cordero Estante Asado
page 49
Hot Pepper and Mint Jellies
or

Steak Relleno
page 73
or

Huachinango a la Ruben
pages 56-57

Piñón Spinach
page 100

Bolillos
page 108

Mixed Green Salad with Jicama, Orange, and Onion
Lista's House Dressing
page 106

Peras al Vino
page 116

Café Mexicano
page 124

Glossary of Southwestern Foods

Adobo Sauce — A piquant sauce of tomato, vinegar, and spices.

Arroz — Rice, which is often served with beans in Southwestern cuisine. We season it with spices, tomatoes, onions and peppers for the traditional Spanish rice.

Bell Peppers — Originating from the Capsicum frutescens family of vegetables, sweet bell peppers are related to chiles but lack the ingredient which makes them "hot." They are available year round in green, yellow, red, and purple varieties, with red and yellow being the sweetest flavor. Where color is not specified, use the green variety.

Burrito — Fresh flour tortilla, rolled and stuffed with beans, meats, or other delicacies.

Carne — Meat. Refers to any meat dish. We use only certified Angus beef.

Cayenne Pepper — Ground form made from dried red cayenne chile peppers.

Cilantro — A cousin to parsley which is popular in Asian as well as Southwestern cooking. Its clean, distinctive taste accents the rich flavors of meats, salsas, and beans.

Chile Relleno — Translates literally into "stuffed chiles." Usually a long chile such as a poblano or a New Mexico chile is stuffed with cheese and finished with a light egg coating.

Chiles — A variety of often misunderstood vegetables, essential to Southwestern cuisine. Their reputations may be red-hot, but many are actually quite sweet. We use them for flavor as much as for heat. Jalapeño, ancho, pasilla, chilpotle, Anaheim, and serrano peppers are among the most commonly used in Southwestern kitchens (see list of peppers).

Chili Powder — A mixture of ground, dried red peppers blended with other spices and herbs. Most brands include dried cumin and oregano as part of the blend. Often the formula may contain paprika, coriander (cilantro), and salt. Legend suggests the first chili powder was invented by Texan, Willie Gebhardt, in 1892.

Chili Verde — A green version of the stew-like recipe. In our recipe, we use diced pork, cooked with hot and mild-spiced green chiles, garlic, and tomatoes.

Chimichanga — A large, overstuffed deep-fried burrito.

Chocolate — Originating in Mexico with the Aztecs. Unsweetened, chocolate is sometimes added to Mexican and Southwestern recipes. Chocolate made its way from America to Europe via the conquistadors. Later it was brought to the United States (then colonies) by colonists. Block Mexican chocolate sold in specialty food stores frequently contains cinnamon, vanilla, cloves, and ground almonds or almond flavoring.

Chorizo — A spicy Mexican-style sausage — we prepare our recipe on premises which includes more than a dozen spices and chiles.

Cinnamon — Often used in Mexican and Southwestern cuisines. Originating from Ceylon, it is available in ground form or in tightly-rolled dry quilts as stick cinnamon.

Coriander — Related to cilantro, this spice is the seed of the plant which gives us the herb. With a dusky flavor, it may be purchased in ground form or as whole dried seeds.

Corn Husks — Dried husks, softened in water, are used as wrappers for some foods such as tamales. The husks form a natural jacket which holds a mixture together while it is steam-cooking.

Cornmeal — A staple of Mexican and Southwestern cooking made from dried corn, originally called maize.

Cumin — A powerful spice, sometimes dominating, often used in traditional Mexican and Southwestern cooking. Available as a whole seed or in ground form. Use sparingly.

Enchiladas — Corn tortillas, rolled or stacked, and baked with beef, chicken, or cheese as a filling and topped with an enchilada sauce.

Fajitas — Refers to a cut of beef also known as the skirt steak. The name has come to encompass the whole fajita and fixin's experience, which we've extended to include chicken, pork, seafood, and vegetables as well as beef.

Frijoles (Beans) — Used extensively in Mexican and Southwestern cooking. Usually refers to dried pinto beans, which are speckled with brown on a pale pinkish background or sometimes black beans which are small, black in color, with a hearty flavor.

Frijoles Charro — Cooked whole pinto beans seasoned with chorizo and fresh cilantro.

Ground red chiles — Pure chile powder, not to be confused with blended chili powder, originates from finely ground dried red chile peppers. Sometimes referred to as ground (dried) hot red pepper.

Guacamole — A piquant mixture of mashed fresh avocado, diced, ripe tomatoes, chiles, and spices. It is an excellent appetizer served with cocktails or other cold beverages, and accompanied by crisp tortilla chips. It is also used as a cool dressing on a variety of dishes.

Herbs — We give the measurement for both fresh and dried herbs in our recipes. Although dried herbs are easily available year round, do not hesitate to use fresh herbs when they're available. The flavor is very rewarding to the result of the finished recipe. You will have to use approximately double the amount of fresh to dried herbs, depending on the intensity of the flavor of the fresh herbs.

Hominy — Dried corn kernels which have been soaked and lightly cooked so that the outer coating can be removed.

Lettuce — For the most part, cold iceberg lettuce is readily available, although leaf lettuce, romaine, and spinach contain more vitamins and provide more color. Use them mostly in salads or as a garnish for tacos or tostadas. Thinly shred the lettuce. When using fresh iceberg to top off or decorate a plate, cut in large strips or tear the leaves into bite-size pieces. Remember a knife or slicer bruises the lettuce leaves. If you are preparing small quantities, opt for quality and presentation rather than speed.

Mangoes — A semi-tropical oval-shaped fruit with a skin in hues of gold, pink, and green, and a deep yellow flesh which is juicy and richly perfumed.

Masa — Literally means "dough" in Spanish. Made from dried corn kernels which have been softened in a lime (calcium hydroxide) solution, the corn is ground and made into cornmeal dough. Fresh masa is commercially available in Mexico and some U.S. specialty food stores; however, it is tricky to work with and dries out easily. It is the main ingredient in tortillas.

Onions — I suggest white (Bermuda) or yellow (Spanish) onions be used for cooking. While the red onion is more pleasing to the eye, it should be used in cold dishes or as a garnish (salads, cold soups, ceviche, etc.).

Pico de Gallo — Literally translated, this means "Rooster's Beak." Better for you to think of it as the classic relish, made with tomatoes, serrano peppers, onions, and spices, and eaten anywhere on anything — except dessert.

Piloncillo — Unrefined sugar available in hard cones. Similar to brown sugar, it is deeper in color with a more pronounced molasses flavor.

Piñóns (pinenuts) — The seeds of the piñón pine tree. They are excellent tasting either raw or toasted. Store tightly covered in the refrigerator or freezer.

Plantain — A larger relative of the banana which is often cooked as a vegetable substitute. Thoroughly ripe sweet plantains will have a black skin.

Quesadilla — A flour tortilla stuffed with cheese and chiles and grilled. Similar to a grilled queso sandwich, only better.

Queso — Means cheese, usually refers to Cheddar or Monterey Jack. Traditional Mexican cheeses were made with goat's or sheep's milk. We have used Monterey Jack or sharp Cheddar in place of the goat cheeses; however, a variety of hard goat cheeses could be substituted.

Salsas — Spanish for sauces, relishes, and/or chutneys. Basically include chopped raw vegetables or fruits combined with fresh herbs, and just enough liquid to hold the mixture together. Serving Salsas has become a hot trend for the 90's that we've been practicing for years.

Taco — A crisp corn tortilla, folded and filled with a variety of fillings.

Tamale — Cornmeal dough topped with a variety of fillings, wrapped in softened dried corn husks, and steam-cooked.

Tequila — A pale, sharp-tasting liquor distilled from the agone plant which grows in a hot dry climate.

Tomatillo — Fat, round, small vegetables the size of large cherry tomatoes, tomatillos grow in papery husks and taste best when they turn a bright green color. They may be used cooked or raw after removing the husks and sticky residue.

Tomatoes — The basis of many Southwestern-style sauces and other recipes. To peel tomatoes, immerse the tomatoes in the boiling water for approximately 30 seconds. While still warm, slide or peel the skin from the tomato. If the peel does not come off easily, immerse tomato for an additional 30 seconds.

Tortillas — The bread of the Southwest, made with flour or cornmeal. They are the basis of Mexican cookery. Tortillas are rolled, folded, used as dippers, crisply fried, and munched with or without the accompaniment of dip or spread. Commercially-made tortillas of both kinds are best stored in the freezer until needed.

Tostada — A crisp flour tortilla, layered with beans, meats, cheese, and vegetables, served open-faced.

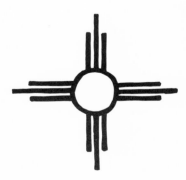

Southwestern-style and Mexican Food and Spice Product Availability Sources

Arizona

Flores Bakery
8402 S. Aucnida del Vaqui
Guadalupe, AZ   85283
(602) 831-9709

Latolteca
1205 E. Van Buren
Phoenix, AZ   85304
(602) 253-1511

Santa Cruz Chile
P.O. Box 177
Tumacacori, AZ   85640
(602) 398-2591

California

El Nopalito Tortilla Factory
560 Santa Fe Drive
Encinitas, CA   92024
(Telephone number not listed)

Chihuahua Tortilleria
718 F Street
Fresno, CA   93706
(Telephone number not listed)

Central Market
Broadway (Downtown)
Los Angeles, CA
(213) 386-1458

Los Cinlo Puntos
3300 Brooklin Avenue
Los Angeles, CA
(213) 261-4084

Mercado del Sol
First Avenue and Lorena
Los Angeles, CA   90063
(213) 265-1966

Mi Rancho
464 Seventh Street
Oakland, CA   94607
(510) 451-2393

Colorado

Casa Herrera
2049 Larimer Street
Denver, CO   80205
(Telephone number not listed)

Jonnies Market
2030 Larimer Street
Denver, CO   80205
(303) 297-0155

La Favorita
3535 Brighton Blvd.
Denver, CO   80216
(303) 295-1625

La Popular
311 Larimer Street
Denver, CO   80204
(303) 296-1672

Connecticut

Gilbertie's Herb Garden
Sylvan Lane
Westport, CT   06705
(203) 227-4175

Hay Day Country Market
1026 Post Road E.
Westport, CT   06880
(203) 227-9008 or 221-0100

Georgia

Rinconcito Latino
2845 Buford Highway, N.E.
Atlanta, GA   30309

Illinois

La Casa del Pueblo
1810 S. Blue Island Avenue
Chicago, IL   60608
(312) 421-4640

Supermercado del Rey
1714 W. 18th Street
Chicago, IL   60608
(Telephone number not listed)

Massachusetts

Garcia Superette
367 Centro Avenue
Jamica Plain, MA   02130
(Telephone number not listed)

Ricardo y Maria's Tortilla
30 Germania Street
Jamica Plain, MA   02130
(Telephone number not listed)

Michigan

Honey Bee La Colmena Supermercado
Bagley at 17th Street
Detroit, MI 48216
(313) 237-0295

Minnesota

El Burrito Mexican Foods
196 Concord Street
St. Paul, MN 55107
(612) 227-2192

Missouri

Tropicanna Market
5001 Lindenwood Ave.
St. Louis, MO 63109
(314) 353-7328

New Mexico

Fruit Basket
3821 12th Street NW
Albuquerque, NM 87107
(505) 345-3942

Hatch Chile Express
622 Franklin
P.O. Box 350
Hatch, NM 87937
(505) 267-3226

Chili Shop, The
109 E. Water
Santa Fe, NM 87501
(505) 983-6080

Green Chili Fix, The
P.O. Box 5463
Santa Fe, NM 87502
(Telephone number not listed)

Roybal Store
216 Galisteo Street
Santa Fe, NM 87501
(Telephone number not listed)

New York

La Marqueta
1607 Park Avenue
New York, NY 10029
(212) 568-1974

Latin American Grocery
2565 Broadway
New York, NY 10025
(Telephone number not listed)

Pennsylvania

La Cantina Provisions
211 N. American St.
Philadelphia, PA 19106
(215) 425-8280

Texas

Caliente Chile Inc.
P.O. Drawer 5340
Austin, TX 78763
(Telephone number not listed)

Sam Lewis & Associates
704 First Savings Bldg.
San Angelo, TX 76901
(915) 658-1432
(Jalapeño lollipops)

Alamo Masa
1603 N. Laredo
San Antonio, TX 78209
(512) 732-9651

El Mercado
612 W. Commerce
San Antonio, TX 78207
(512) 299-8596

El Mercado des Americas
507 E. Commerce
San Antonio, TX 78205
(512) 226-2288

Virgina

Latin Imports
14500 F. Lee Road
Chantilly, VA 22021
(Greater Washington, D.C.)
(703) 631-8825/26
FAX: (703) 631-8865

Chef Garcia Tortilleria
7608 S. Fullerton Road
Springfield, VA 22153
(Greater Washington, D.C.)
(Telephone number not listed)

La Tienda
190 Boggs Avenue
Virginia Beach, VA 23452
(804) 340-3613

INDEX